Oh My Goddess!

あ女神こあ

adventures of the
Mini-Goddesses

STORY AND ART BY

Kosuke Fujishima

TRANSLATION BY

Dana Lewis
& Toren Smith

LETTERING
AND TOUCH-UP BY

Susie Lee
& PC Orz

with Tom Orzechowski
and L. Lois Buhalis

DARK HORSE MANGA™

PUBLISHER
Mike Richardson

SERIES EDITOR
Rachel Penn

COLLECTION EDITOR
Chris Warner

COLLECTION DESIGNER
Amy Arendts

ART DIRECTOR
Mark Cox

English-language edition produced by Studio Proteus for Dark Horse Comics, Inc.

OH MY GODDESS! Adventures of the Mini-Goddesses

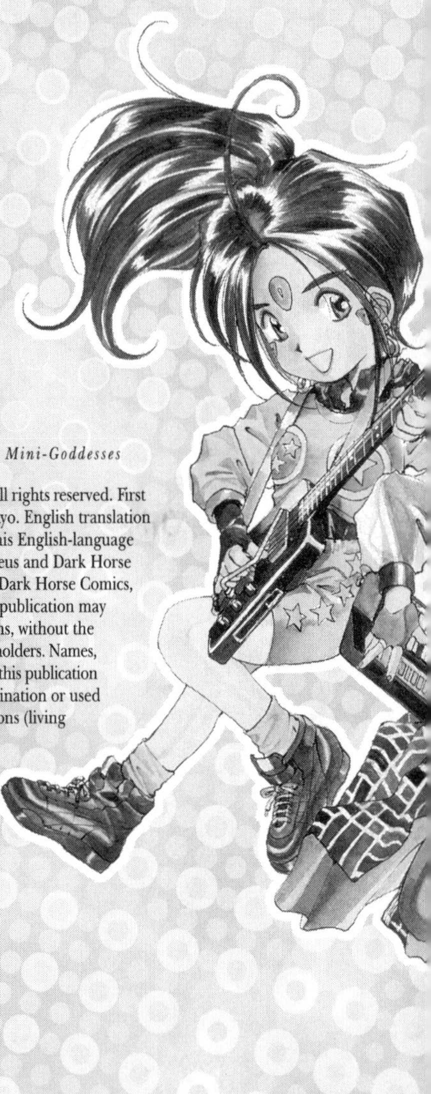

Published by Dark Horse Manga
A division of Dark Horse Comics, Inc.
10956 SE Main Street
Milwaukie, OR 97222

darkhorse.com

First edition: May 2000
ISBN: 1-56971-421-5

10 9 8 7 6 5 4
Printed in Canada

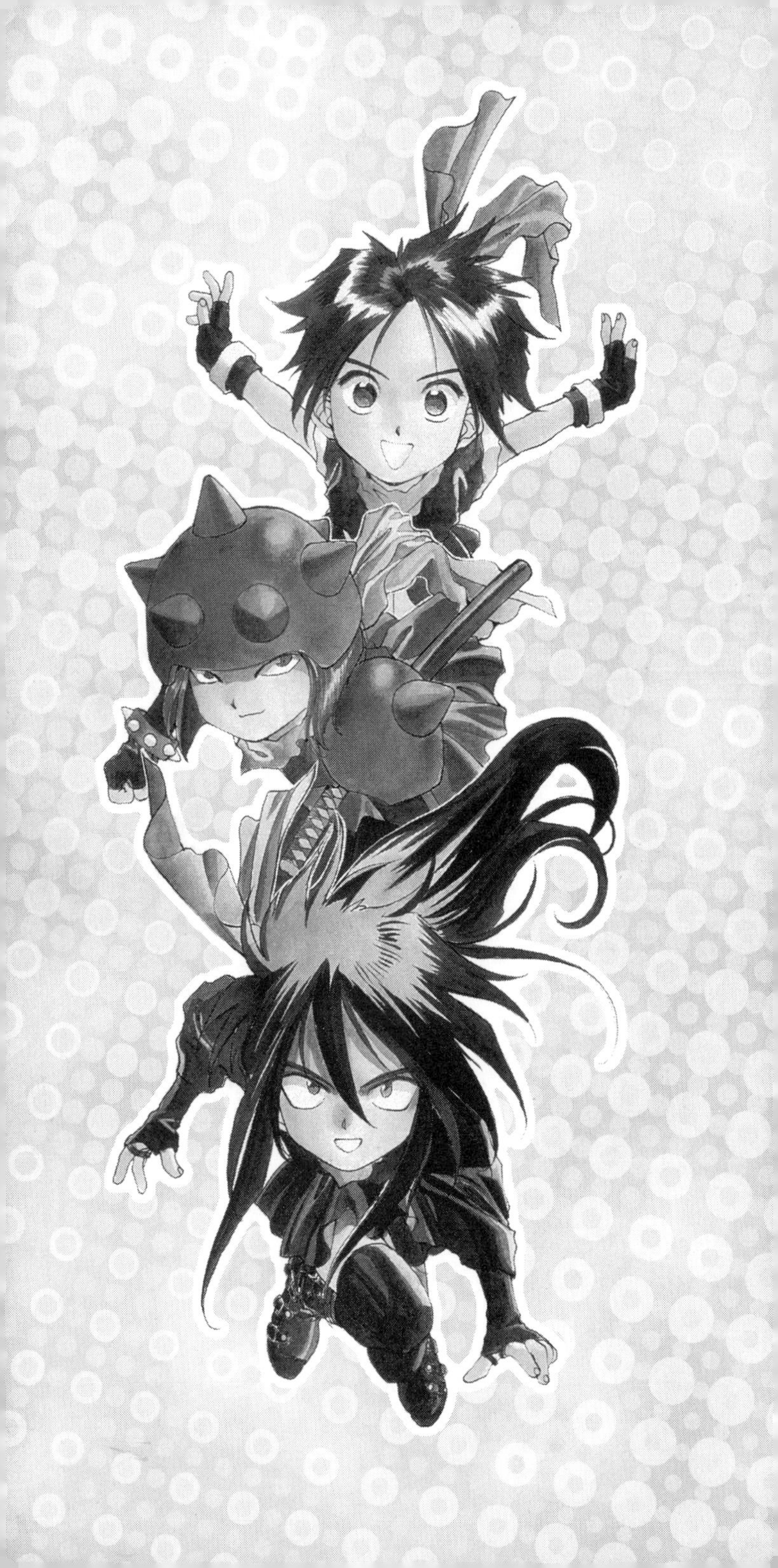

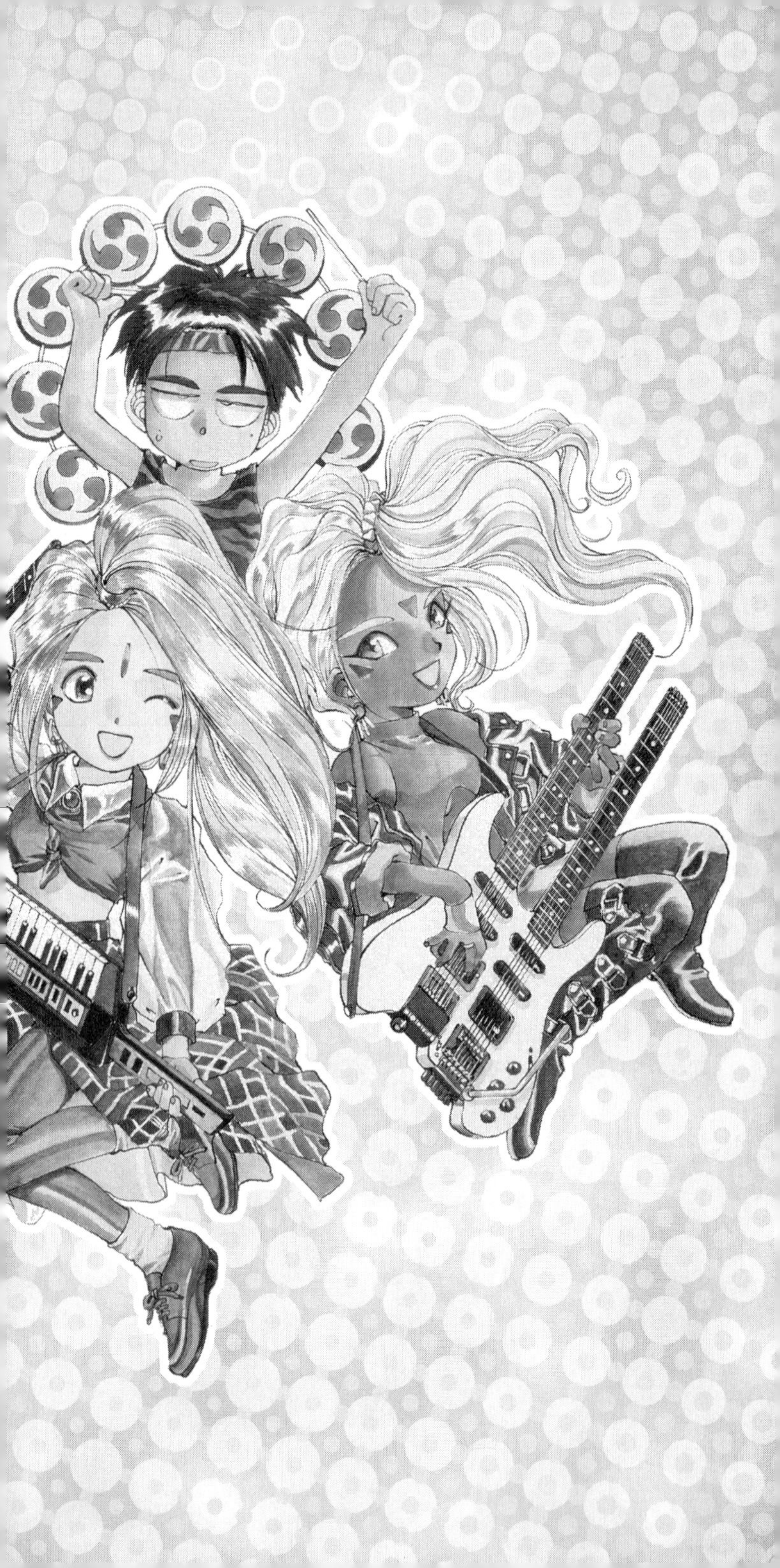

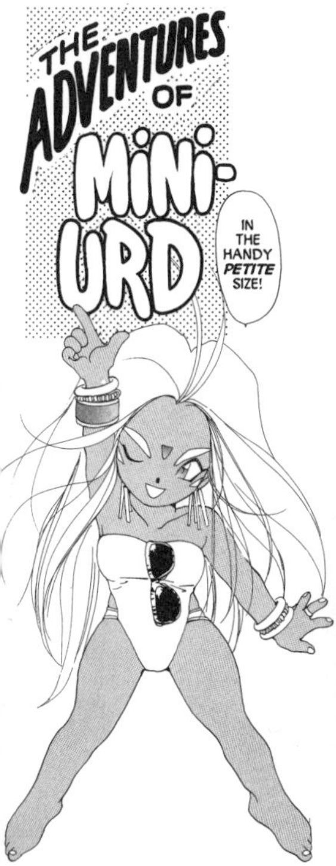
THE ADVENTURES OF MINI-URD
IN THE HANDY *PETITE* SIZE!

HOUSEHOLD EXPEDITION

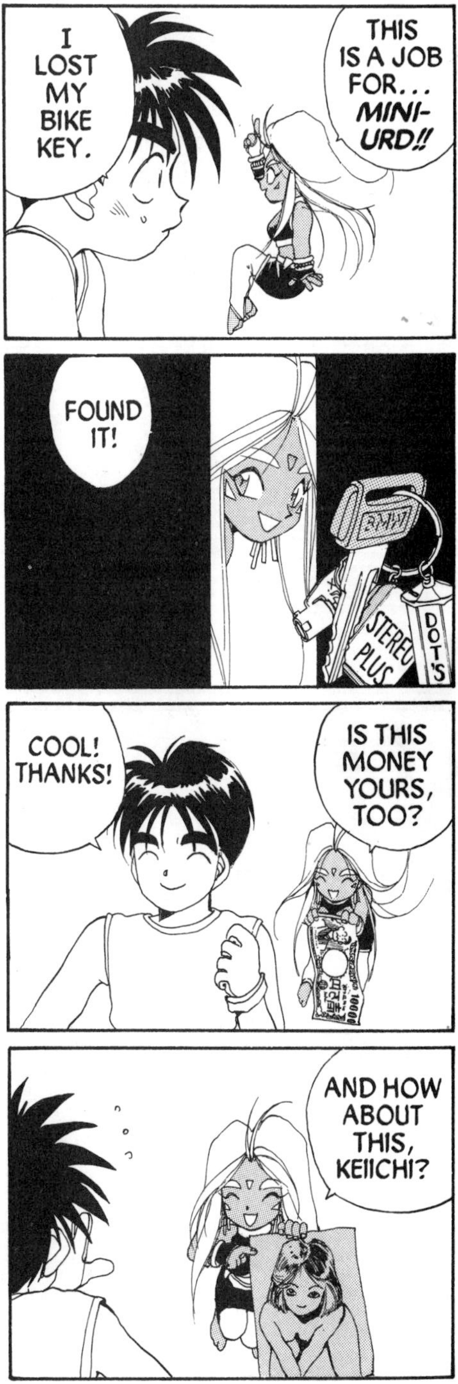
I LOST MY BIKE KEY.
THIS IS A JOB FOR... *MINI-URD!!*
FOUND IT!
BMW
STEREO PLUS
DOT'S
COOL! THANKS!
IS THIS MONEY YOURS, TOO?
AND HOW ABOUT THIS, KEIICHI?

VACATION

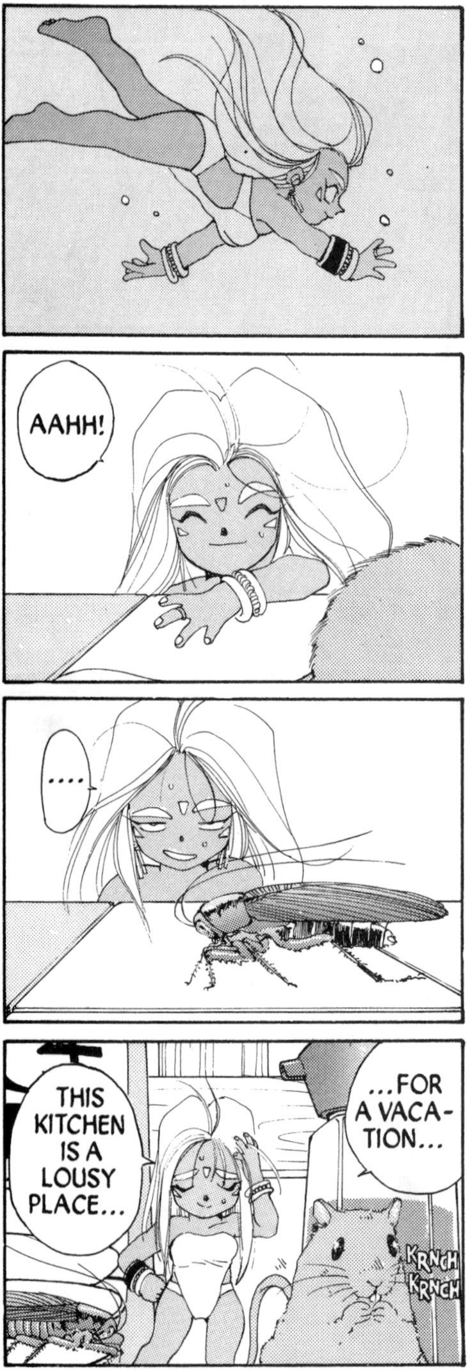
AAHH!
....
THIS KITCHEN IS A LOUSY PLACE...
...FOR A VACATION...
KRNCH KRNCH

ANSWERING SERVICE

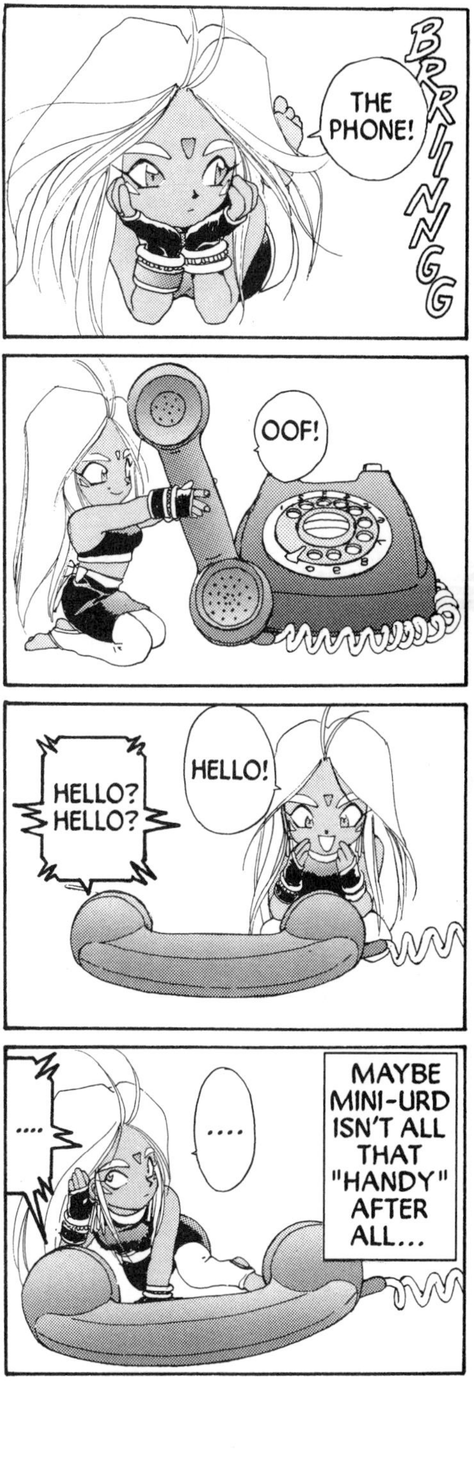
THE PHONE!
BRRIINNGG
OOF!
HELLO? HELLO?
HELLO!
....
....
MAYBE MINI-URD ISN'T ALL THAT "HANDY" AFTER ALL...

URD SOUP

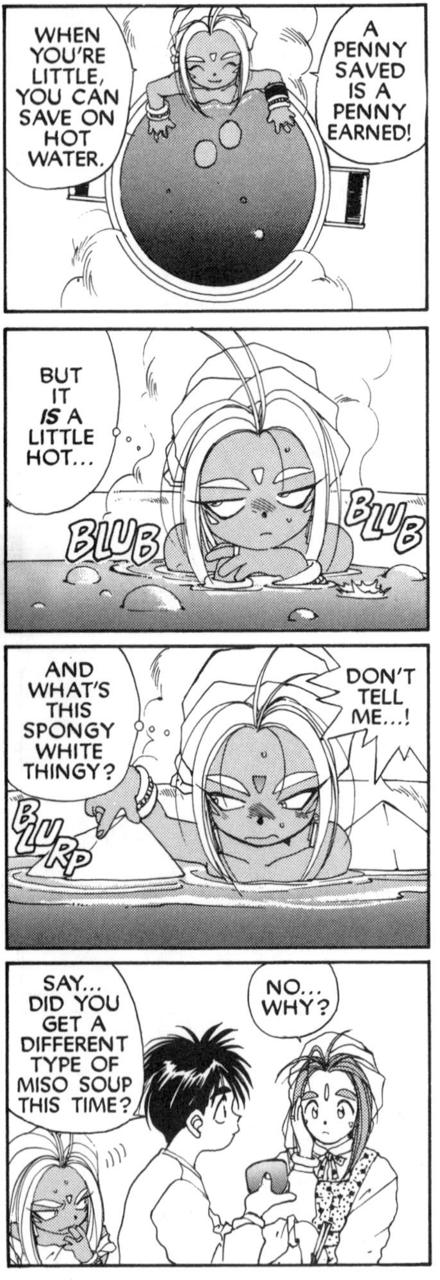
WHEN YOU'RE LITTLE, YOU CAN SAVE ON HOT WATER.
A PENNY SAVED IS A PENNY EARNED!
BUT IT *IS* A LITTLE HOT...
BLUB
BLUB
AND WHAT'S THIS SPONGY WHITE THINGY?
DON'T TELL ME...!
BLURP
SAY... DID YOU GET A DIFFERENT TYPE OF MISO SOUP THIS TIME?
NO... WHY?

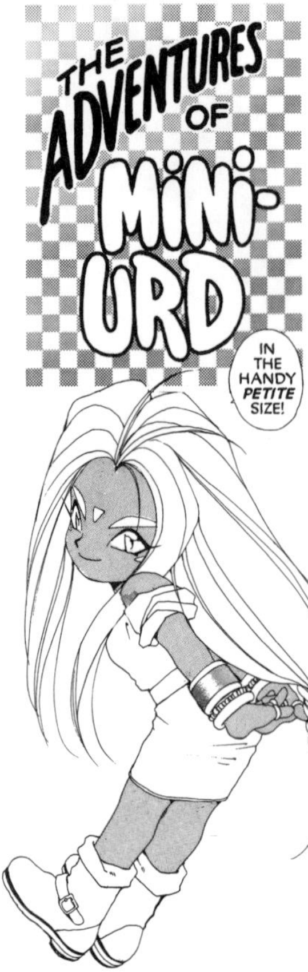
THE ADVENTURES OF MINI-URD
IN THE HANDY *PETITE* SIZE!

1/24

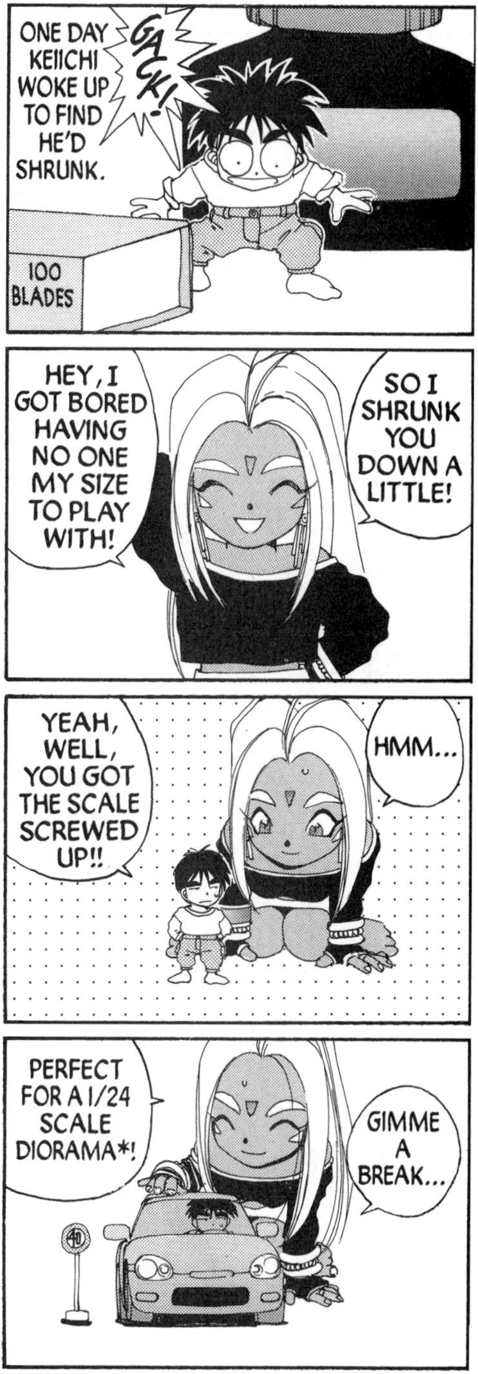
ONE DAY KEIICHI WOKE UP TO FIND HE'D SHRUNK.
GACK!
100 BLADES
HEY, I GOT BORED HAVING NO ONE MY SIZE TO PLAY WITH!
SO I SHRUNK YOU DOWN A LITTLE!
YEAH, WELL, YOU GOT THE SCALE SCREWED UP!!
HMM...
PERFECT FOR A 1/24 SCALE DIORAMA*!
GIMME A BREAK...
40

*: A MINIATURE SCENE DEPICTING FIGURES IN A REALISTIC SETTING

1/35

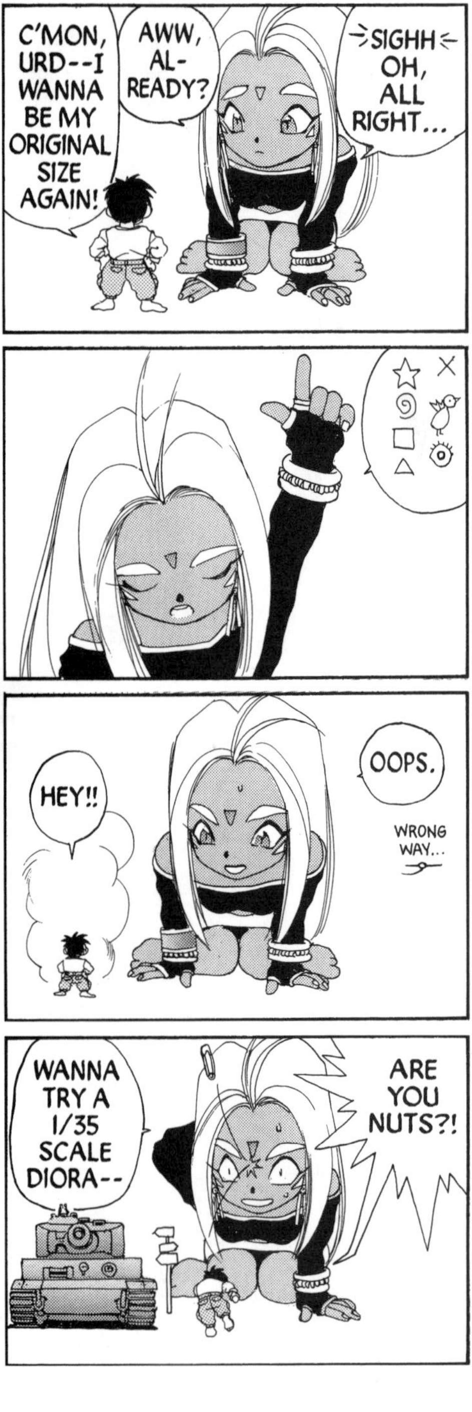
C'MON, URD--I WANNA BE MY ORIGINAL SIZE AGAIN!
AWW, AL-READY?
SIGHH OH, ALL RIGHT...
HEY!!
OOPS.
WRONG WAY...
WANNA TRY A 1/35 SCALE DIORA--
ARE YOU NUTS?!

IT'S THE THOUGHT THAT COUNTS

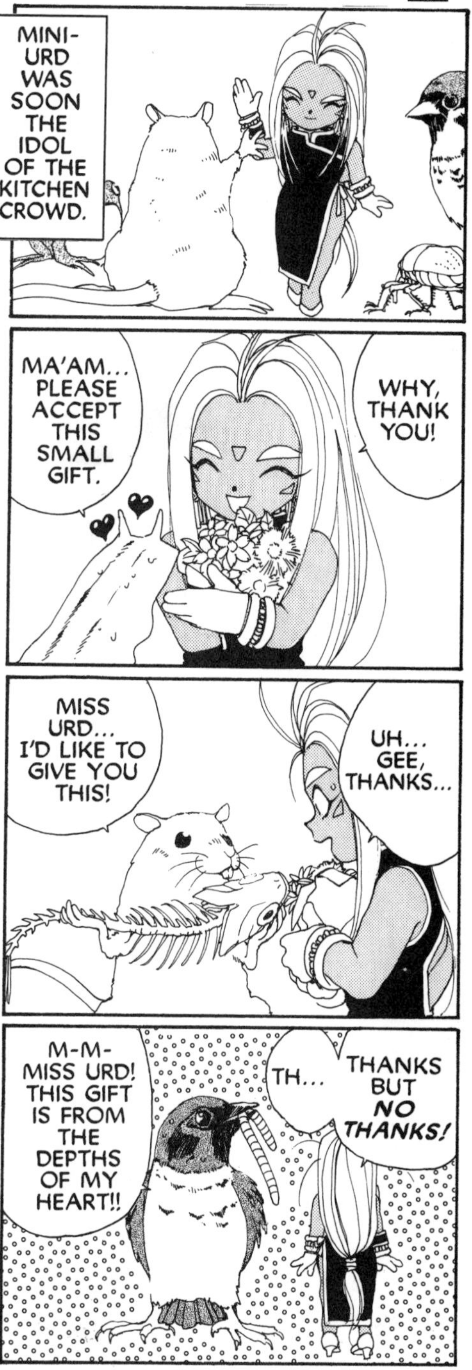

MINI-URD WAS SOON THE IDOL OF THE KITCHEN CROWD.
MA'AM... PLEASE ACCEPT THIS SMALL GIFT.
WHY, THANK YOU!
MISS URD... I'D LIKE TO GIVE YOU THIS!
UH... GEE, THANKS...
M-M-MISS URD! THIS GIFT IS FROM THE DEPTHS OF MY HEART!!
TH...
THANKS BUT ***NO THANKS!***

FAMILY

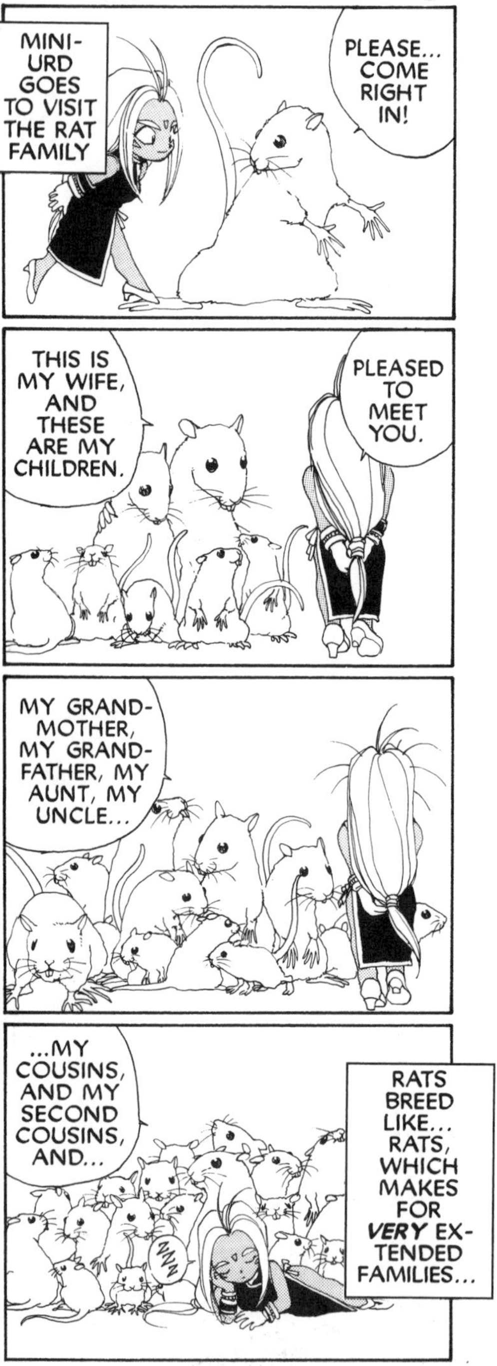
MINI-URD GOES TO VISIT THE RAT FAMILY
PLEASE... COME RIGHT IN!
THIS IS MY WIFE, AND THESE ARE MY CHILDREN.
PLEASED TO MEET YOU.
MY GRAND-MOTHER, MY GRAND-FATHER, MY AUNT, MY UNCLE...
...MY COUSINS, AND MY SECOND COUSINS, AND...
RATS BREED LIKE... RATS, WHICH MAKES FOR *VERY* EX-TENDED FAMILIES...

CELL DIVISION

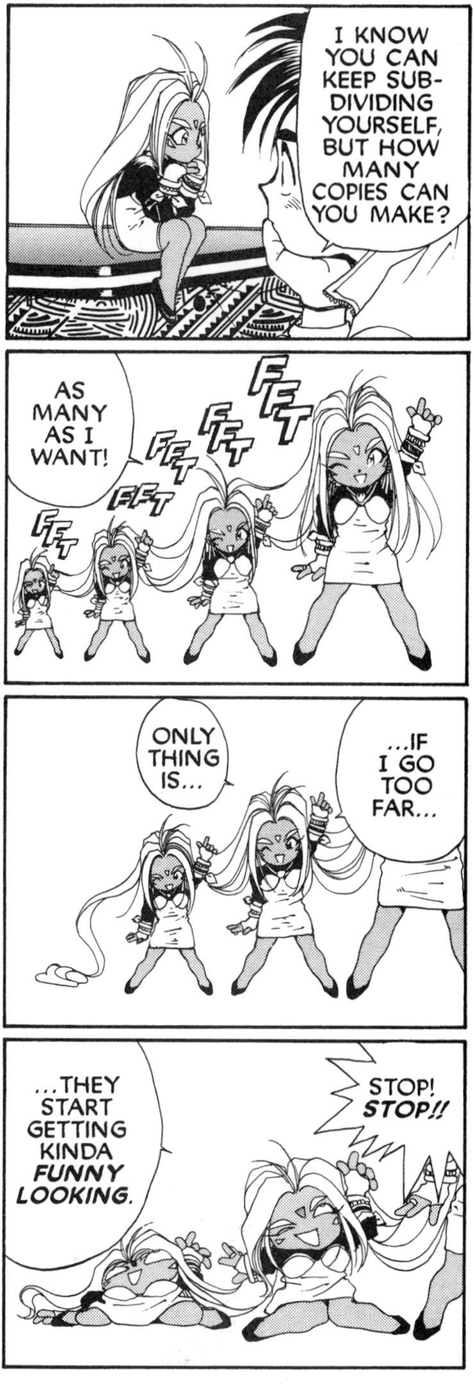
I KNOW YOU CAN KEEP SUB-DIVIDING YOURSELF, BUT HOW MANY COPIES CAN YOU MAKE?
AS MANY AS I WANT!
FFT
FFT
FFT
FFT
FFT
ONLY THING IS...
...IF I GO TOO FAR...
...THEY START GETTING KINDA *FUNNY LOOKING*.
STOP! *STOP!!*

LOST AND FOUND

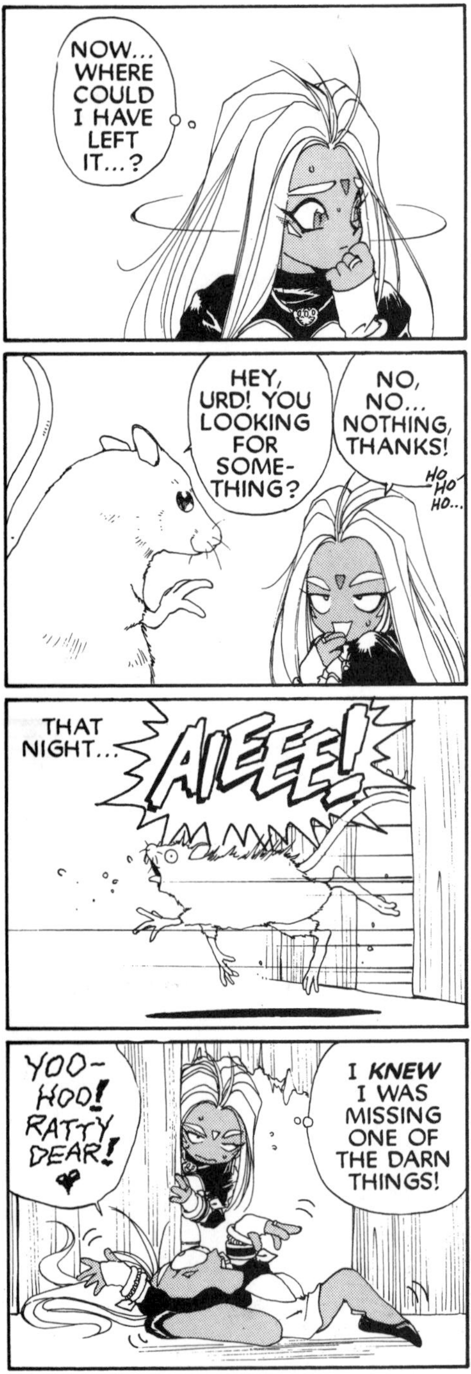
NOW... WHERE COULD I HAVE LEFT IT...?
HEY, URD! YOU LOOKING FOR SOME-THING?
NO, NO... NOTHING, THANKS!
HO HO HO...
THAT NIGHT...
AIEEE!
YOO-HOO! RATTY DEAR!
I *KNEW* I WAS MISSING ONE OF THE DARN THINGS!

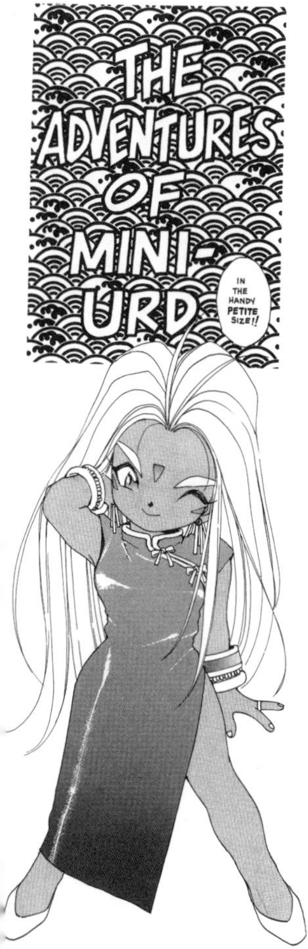
THE ADVENTURES OF MINI-URD
IN THE HANDY PETITE SIZE!!

HEALTH CARE

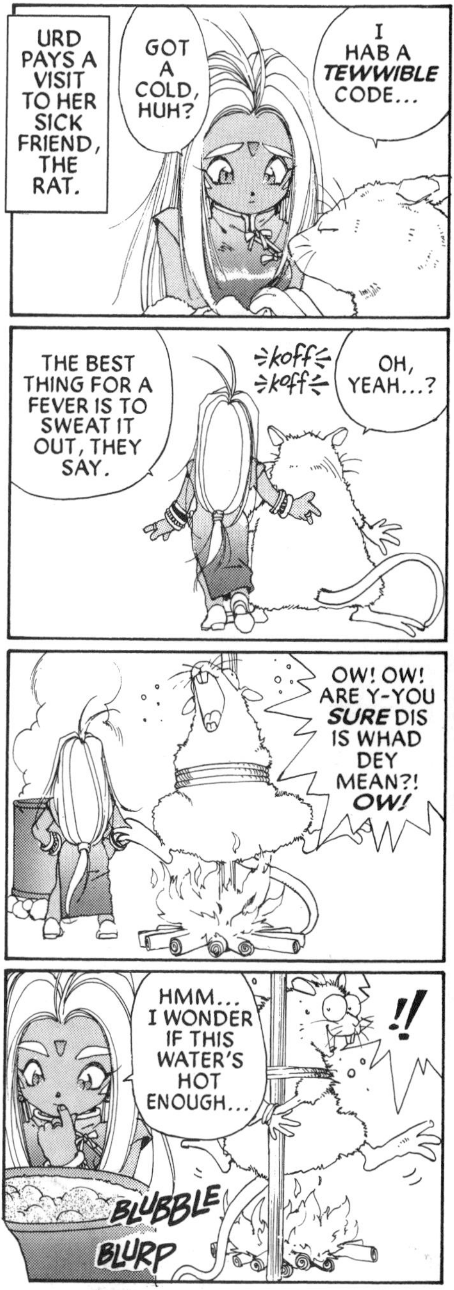
URD PAYS A VISIT TO HER SICK FRIEND, THE RAT.
GOT A COLD, HUH?
I HAB A *TEWWIBLE* CODE...
THE BEST THING FOR A FEVER IS TO SWEAT IT OUT, THEY SAY.
koff koff
OH, YEAH...?
OW! OW! ARE Y-YOU *SURE* DIS IS WHAD DEY MEAN?! *OW!*
HMM... I WONDER IF THIS WATER'S HOT ENOUGH...
!!
BLUBBLE
BLURP

COLD MEDICINE

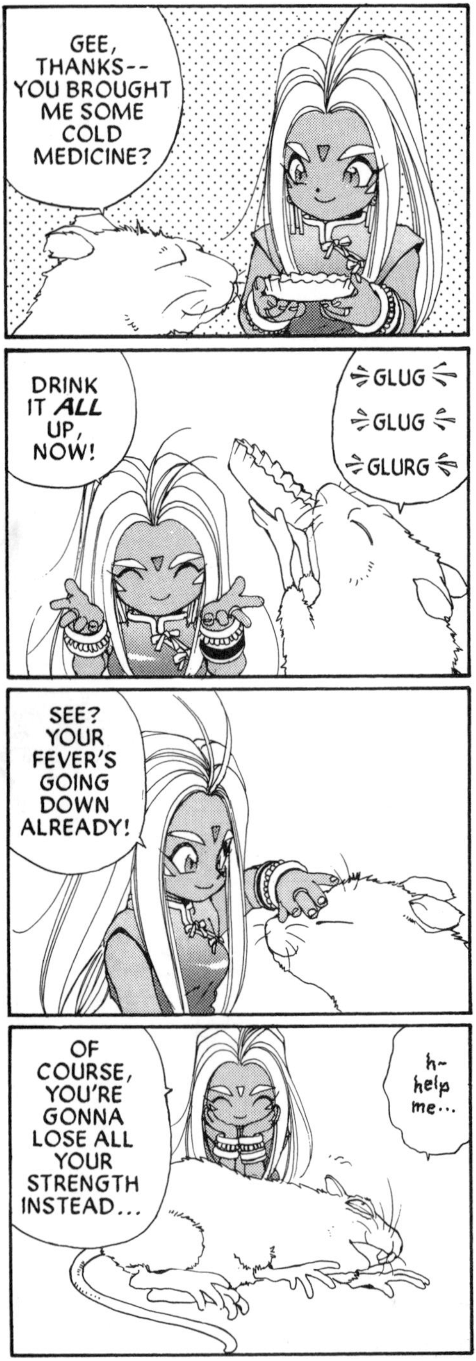
GEE, THANKS-- YOU BROUGHT ME SOME COLD MEDICINE?
DRINK IT ***ALL*** UP, NOW!
GLUG
GLUG
GLURG
SEE? YOUR FEVER'S GOING DOWN ALREADY!
OF COURSE, YOU'RE GONNA LOSE ALL YOUR STRENGTH INSTEAD...
h-help me...

STOMACH MEDICINE

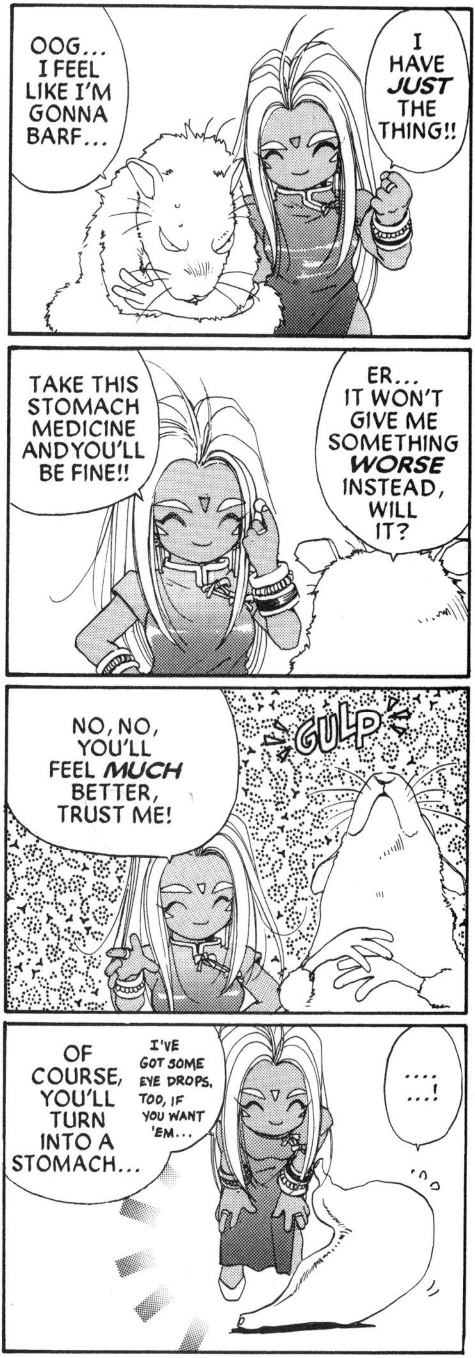

OOG... I FEEL LIKE I'M GONNA BARF...
I HAVE *JUST* THE THING!!
TAKE THIS STOMACH MEDICINE ANDYOU'LL BE FINE!!
ER... IT WON'T GIVE ME SOMETHING *WORSE* INSTEAD, WILL IT?
NO, NO, YOU'LL FEEL *MUCH* BETTER, TRUST ME!
GULP
OF COURSE, YOU'LL TURN INTO A STOMACH...
I'VE GOT SOME EYE DROPS, TOO, IF YOU WANT 'EM...
.....!

TRUST ME!

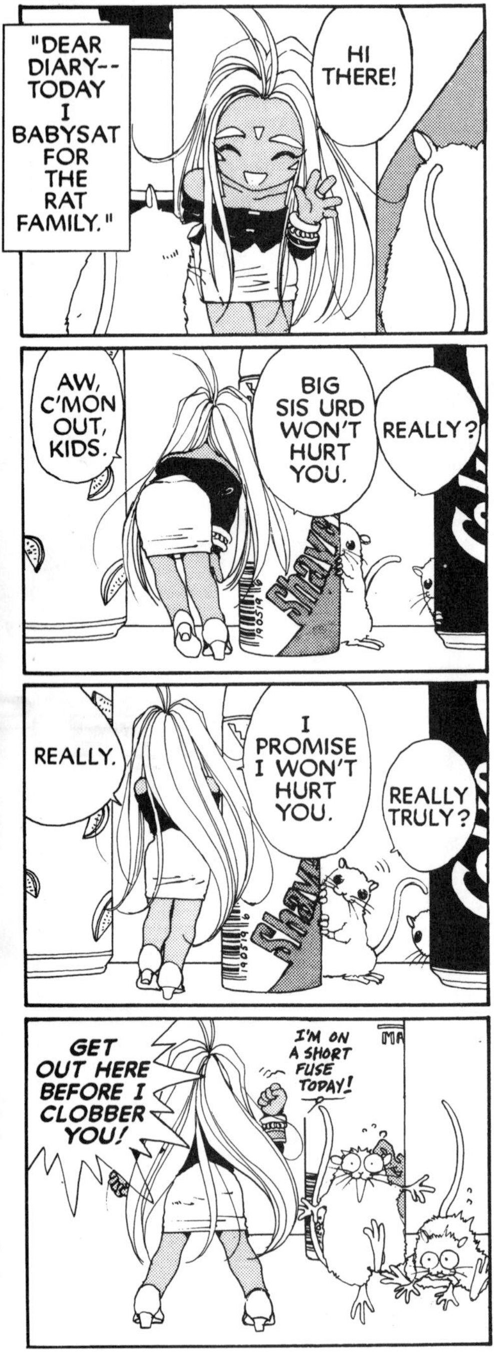
"DEAR DIARY-- TODAY I BABYSAT FOR THE RAT FAMILY."
HI THERE!
AW, C'MON OUT, KIDS.
BIG SIS URD WON'T HURT YOU.
REALLY?
REALLY.
I PROMISE I WON'T HURT YOU.
REALLY TRULY?
GET OUT HERE BEFORE I CLOBBER YOU!
I'M ON A SHORT FUSE TODAY!

GOD OF GAMBLERS

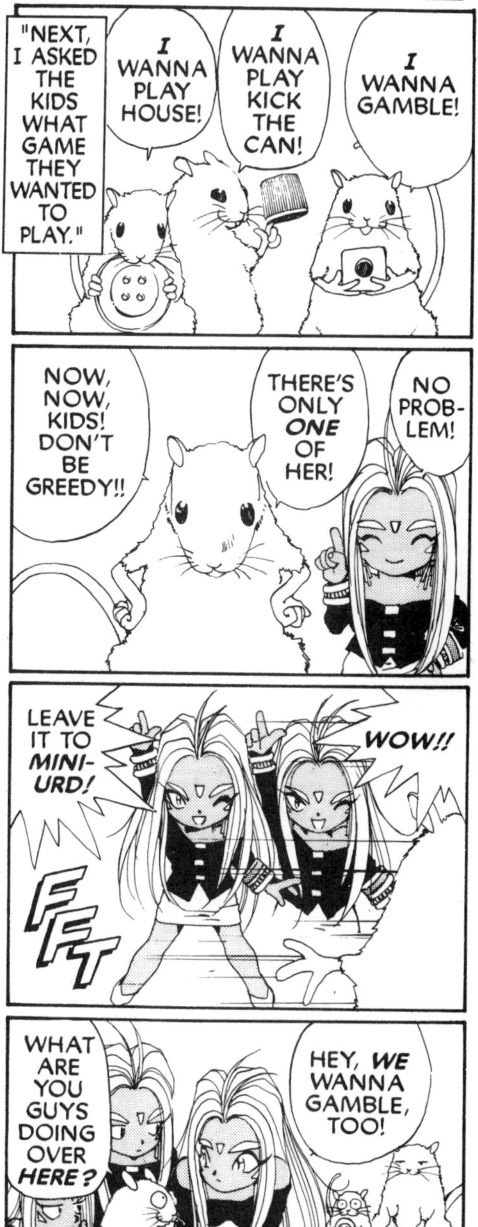
"NEXT, I ASKED THE KIDS WHAT GAME THEY WANTED TO PLAY."
I WANNA PLAY HOUSE!
I WANNA PLAY KICK THE CAN!
I WANNA GAMBLE!
NOW, NOW, KIDS! DON'T BE GREEDY!!
THERE'S ONLY ONE OF HER!
NO PROB-LEM!
LEAVE IT TO MINI-URD!
WOW!!
FFT
WHAT ARE YOU GUYS DOING OVER HERE?
HEY, WE WANNA GAMBLE, TOO!

◊ AMAZING! THE CARDS NEVER LIE! ◊

MINI-URD DECIDED TO TRY HER HAND AT FORTUNE TELLING...
THE CARDS KNOW ALL!
STEP RIGHT UP!
'SCUSE ME, MA'AM, BUT... I WANT TO KNOW WHO MY NEXT GIRLFRIEND WILL BE.
YOUR WISH IS MY COMMAND!
ALA-KAZAM!!
PRESTO!
"PRESTO" ...?
A TEA POT

◊ YOU'RE COVERED! URD'S TOTAL AFTER-SERVICE ◊

TIME PASSED, AND...
THIS CAN'T BE...
HOW CAN I LOVE SOMETHING THAT JUST SITS THERE?
LEAVE IT TO *MINI-URD!*
MORE TEA, HONEY-BUNNY? ♥
THAT DOESN'T MAKE THINGS ANY BETTER!!
GEEZ-- WHAT A COMPLAINER!

SOAKING UP THE RAYS

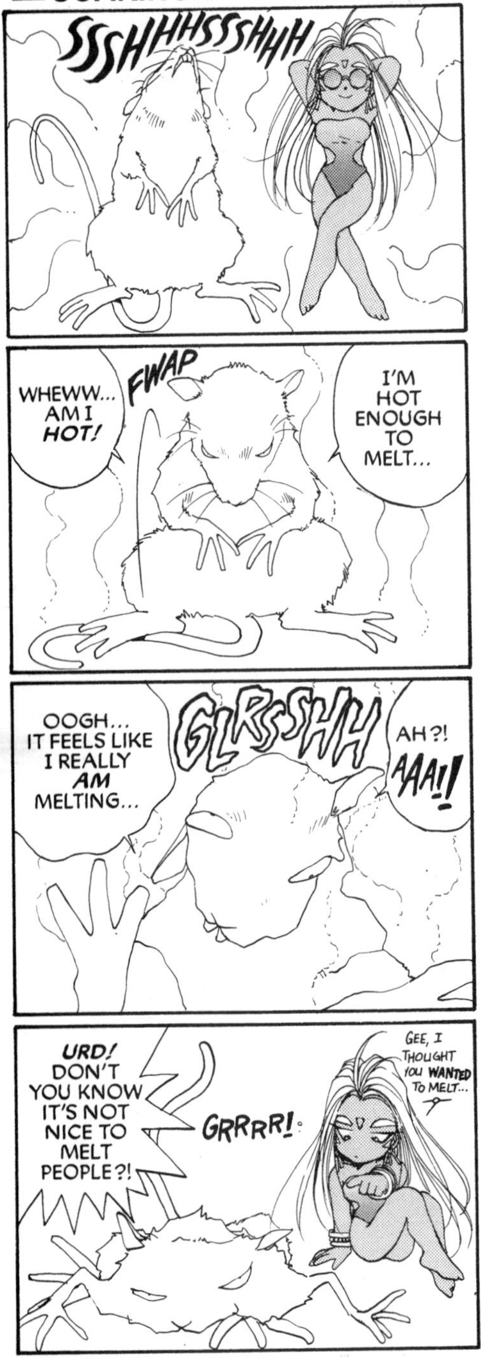
SSSHHHSSSSHHH
WHEWW... AM I HOT!
FWAP
I'M HOT ENOUGH TO MELT...
OOGH... IT FEELS LIKE I REALLY AM MELTING...
GLRSSHH
AH?! AAA!!
URD! DON'T YOU KNOW IT'S NOT NICE TO MELT PEOPLE?!
GRRRR!
GEE, I THOUGHT YOU WANTED TO MELT...

A COOL BREEZE IN SUMMER

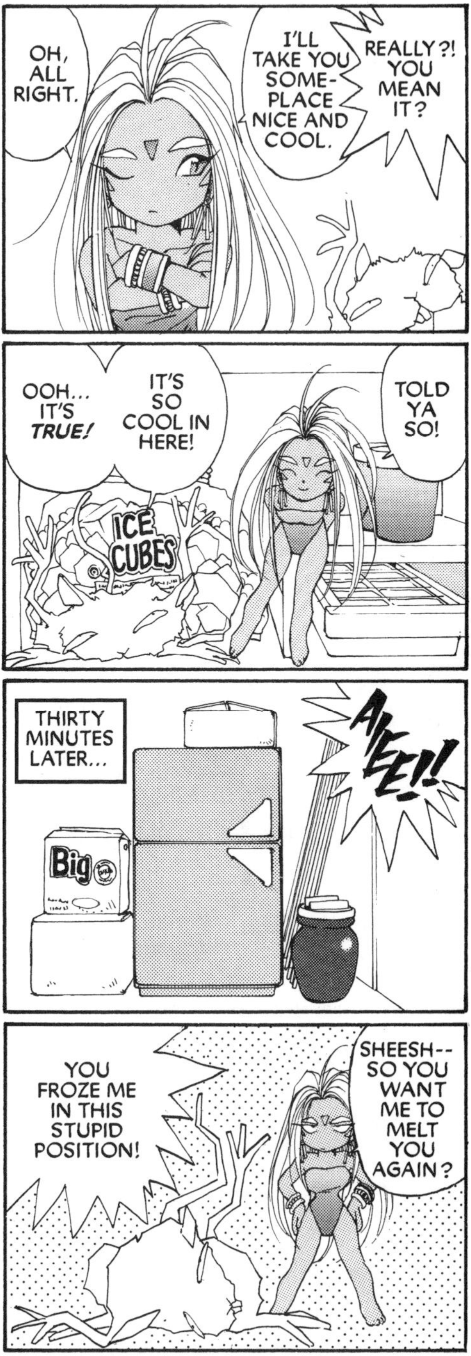

OH, ALL RIGHT.
I'LL TAKE YOU SOME-PLACE NICE AND COOL.
REALLY?! YOU MEAN IT?
OOH... IT'S *TRUE!*
IT'S SO COOL IN HERE!
TOLD YA SO!
ICE CUBES
THIRTY MINUTES LATER...
AIEEE!!
Big
YOU FROZE ME IN THIS STUPID POSITION!
SHEESH-- SO YOU WANT ME TO MELT YOU AGAIN?

THE BIKE MECHANIC AND THE ELVES

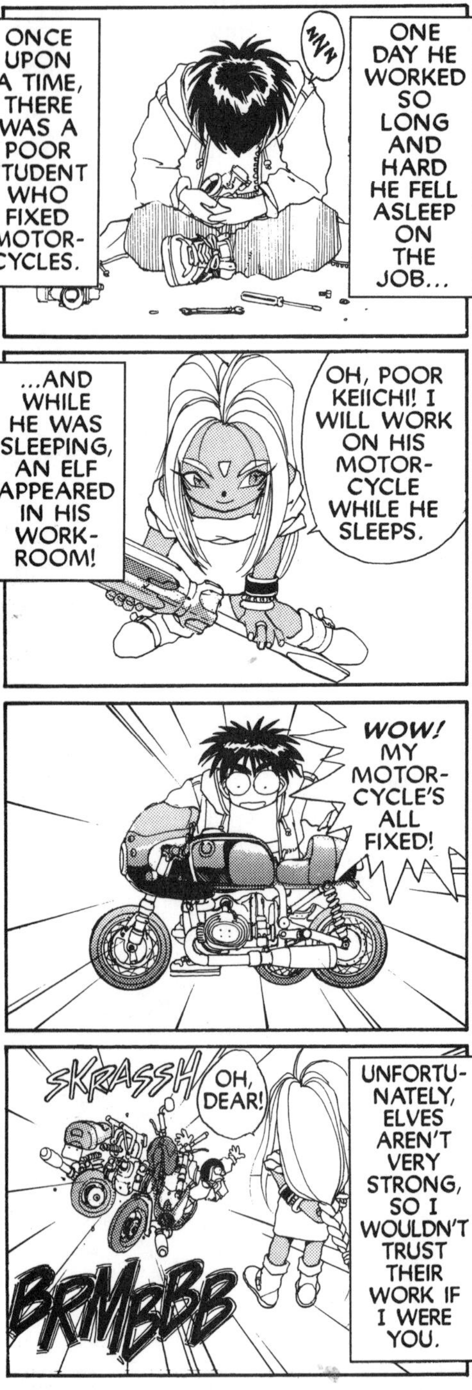
ONCE UPON A TIME, THERE WAS A POOR STUDENT WHO FIXED MOTOR-CYCLES.
MNN
ONE DAY HE WORKED SO LONG AND HARD HE FELL ASLEEP ON THE JOB...
...AND WHILE HE WAS SLEEPING, AN ELF APPEARED IN HIS WORK-ROOM!
OH, POOR KEIICHI! I WILL WORK ON HIS MOTOR-CYCLE WHILE HE SLEEPS.
WOW! MY MOTOR-CYCLE'S ALL FIXED!
SKRASSH
OH, DEAR!
UNFORTU-NATELY, ELVES AREN'T VERY STRONG, SO I WOULDN'T TRUST THEIR WORK IF I WERE YOU.
BRMBBB

TASTY

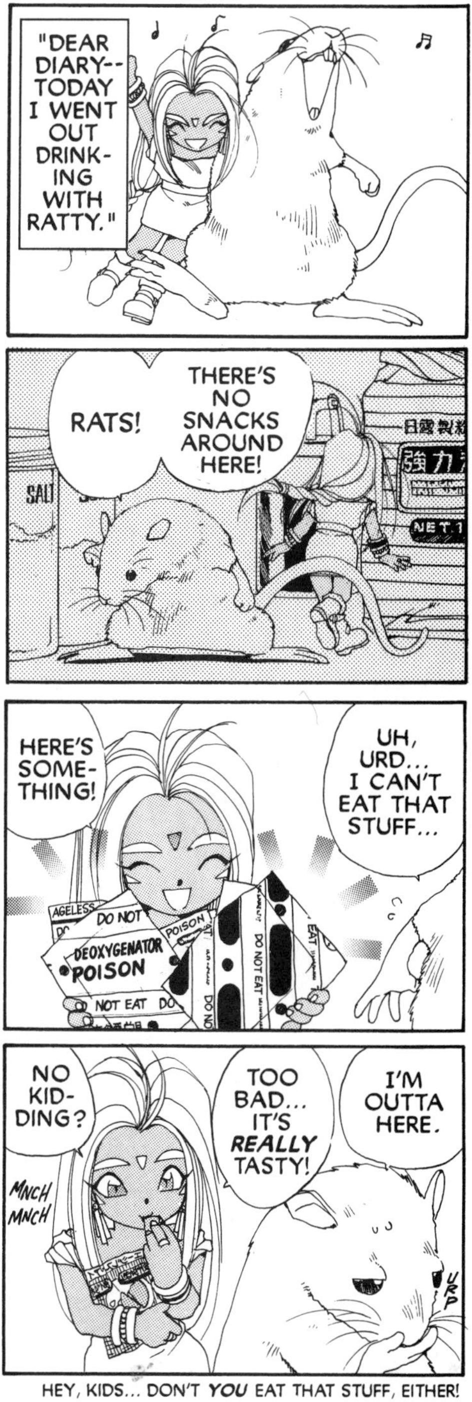
"DEAR DIARY-- TODAY I WENT OUT DRINK-ING WITH RATTY."
RATS!
THERE'S NO SNACKS AROUND HERE!
SALT
HERE'S SOME-THING!
UH, URD... I CAN'T EAT THAT STUFF...
AGELESS
DO NOT
POISON
DEOXYGENATOR
POISON
NOT EAT
DO NOT EAT
NO KID-DING?
TOO BAD... IT'S *REALLY* TASTY!
I'M OUTTA HERE.
MNCH MNCH
URP

HEY, KIDS... DON'T ***YOU*** EAT THAT STUFF, EITHER!

THE CASUAL BET

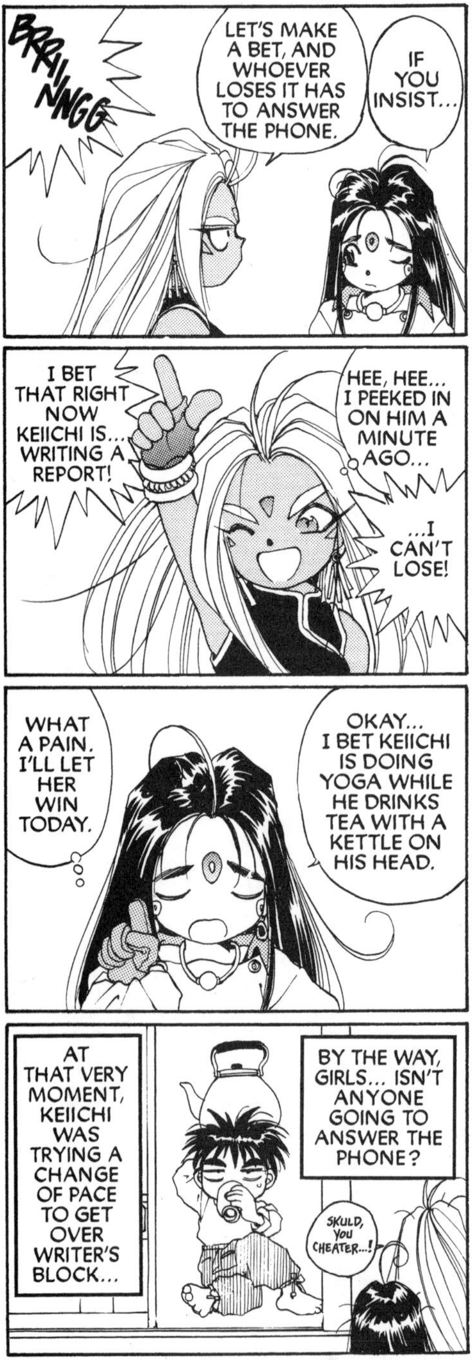
BRRIIINNGG
LET'S MAKE A BET, AND WHOEVER LOSES IT HAS TO ANSWER THE PHONE.
IF YOU INSIST...
I BET THAT RIGHT NOW KEIICHI IS... WRITING A REPORT!
HEE, HEE... I PEEKED IN ON HIM A MINUTE AGO...
...I CAN'T LOSE!
WHAT A PAIN. I'LL LET HER WIN TODAY.
OKAY... I BET KEIICHI IS DOING YOGA WHILE HE DRINKS TEA WITH A KETTLE ON HIS HEAD.
AT THAT VERY MOMENT, KEIICHI WAS TRYING A CHANGE OF PACE TO GET OVER WRITER'S BLOCK...
BY THE WAY, GIRLS... ISN'T ANYONE GOING TO ANSWER THE PHONE?
SKULD, YOU CHEATER...!

CAN YOU EAT THIS?!
◆ THE ULTIMATE GOURMAND! ◆

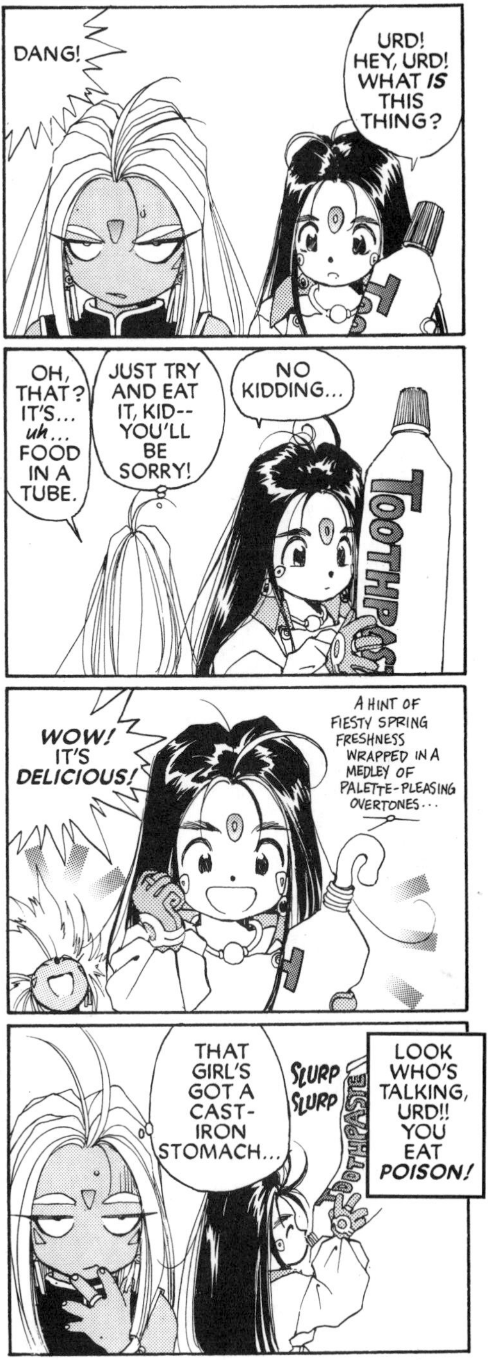
DANG!
URD! HEY, URD! WHAT *IS* THIS THING?
OH, THAT? IT'S... *uh*... FOOD IN A TUBE.
JUST TRY AND EAT IT, KID-- YOU'LL BE SORRY!
NO KIDDING...
WOW! IT'S *DELICIOUS!*
A HINT OF FIESTY SPRING FRESHNESS WRAPPED IN A MEDLEY OF PALETTE-PLEASING OVERTONES...
THAT GIRL'S GOT A CAST-IRON STOMACH...
SLURP SLURP
LOOK WHO'S TALKING, URD!! YOU EAT *POISON!*

WAKE-UP CALL

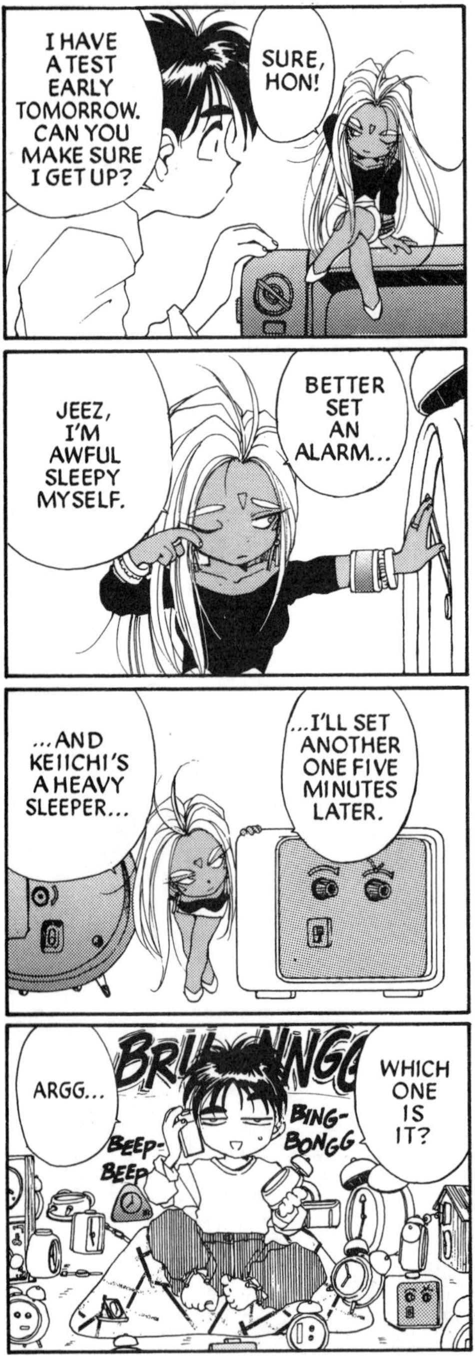
I HAVE A TEST EARLY TOMORROW. CAN YOU MAKE SURE I GET UP?
SURE, HON!
JEEZ, I'M AWFUL SLEEPY MYSELF.
BETTER SET AN ALARM...
...AND KEIICHI'S A HEAVY SLEEPER...
...I'LL SET ANOTHER ONE FIVE MINUTES LATER.
ARGG...
BEEP-BEEP
BING-BONGG
WHICH ONE IS IT?

JUST ONE OF THOSE DAYS

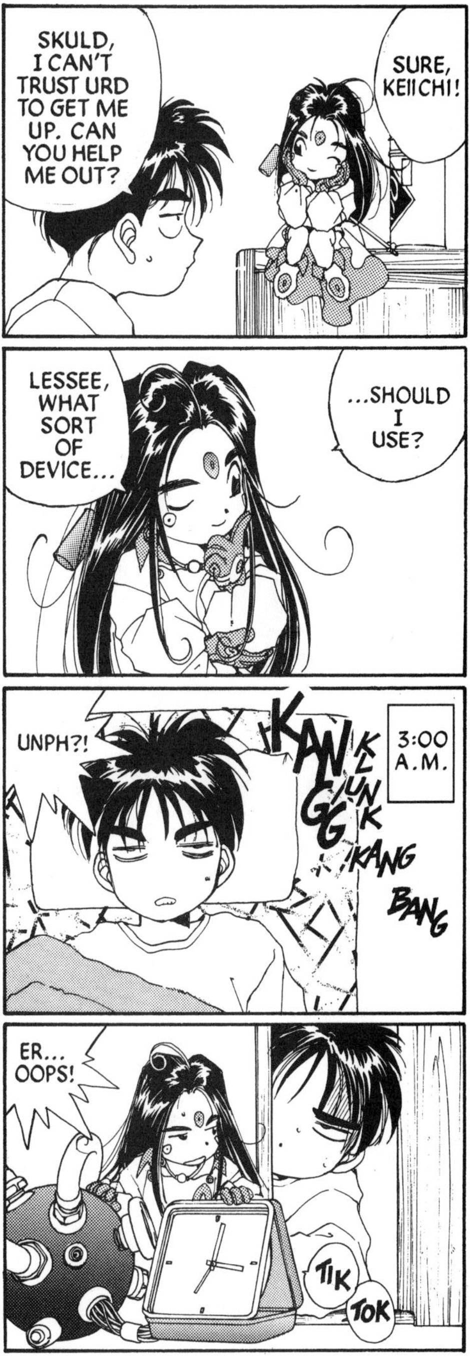
SKULD, I CAN'T TRUST URD TO GET ME UP. CAN YOU HELP ME OUT?
SURE, KEIICHI!
LESSEE, WHAT SORT OF DEVICE...
...SHOULD I USE?
UNPH?!
KANGG
KLUNK
3:00 A.M.
KANG
BANG
ER... OOPS!
TIK
TOK

THE GREAT SLUG RACE

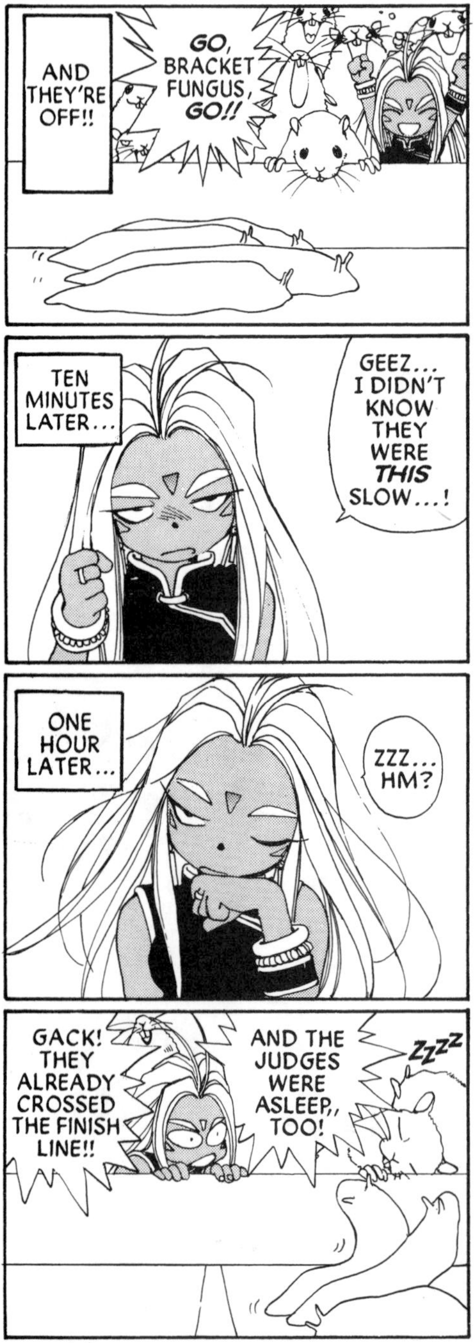
AND THEY'RE OFF!!
GO, BRACKET FUNGUS, GO!!
TEN MINUTES LATER...
GEEZ... I DIDN'T KNOW THEY WERE THIS SLOW...!
ONE HOUR LATER...
ZZZ... HM?
GACK! THEY ALREADY CROSSED THE FINISH LINE!!
AND THE JUDGES WERE ASLEEP,, TOO!
ZZZZ

THE GREAT CRICKET RACE

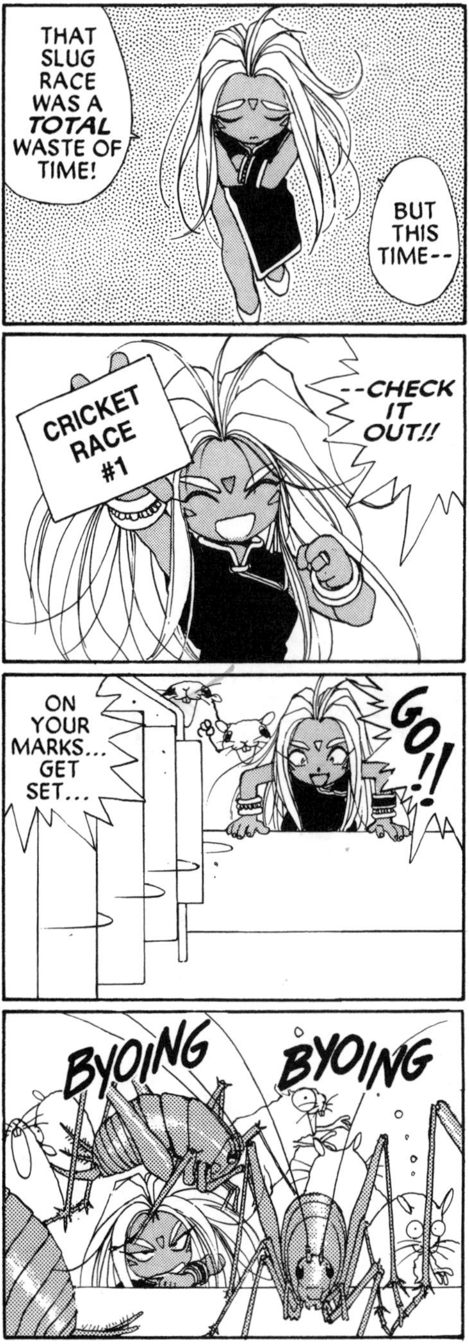
THAT SLUG RACE WAS A *TOTAL* WASTE OF TIME!
BUT THIS TIME--
CRICKET RACE #1
--CHECK IT OUT!!
ON YOUR MARKS... GET SET...
GO!!
BYOING
BYOING

GOLDEN GOURMAND

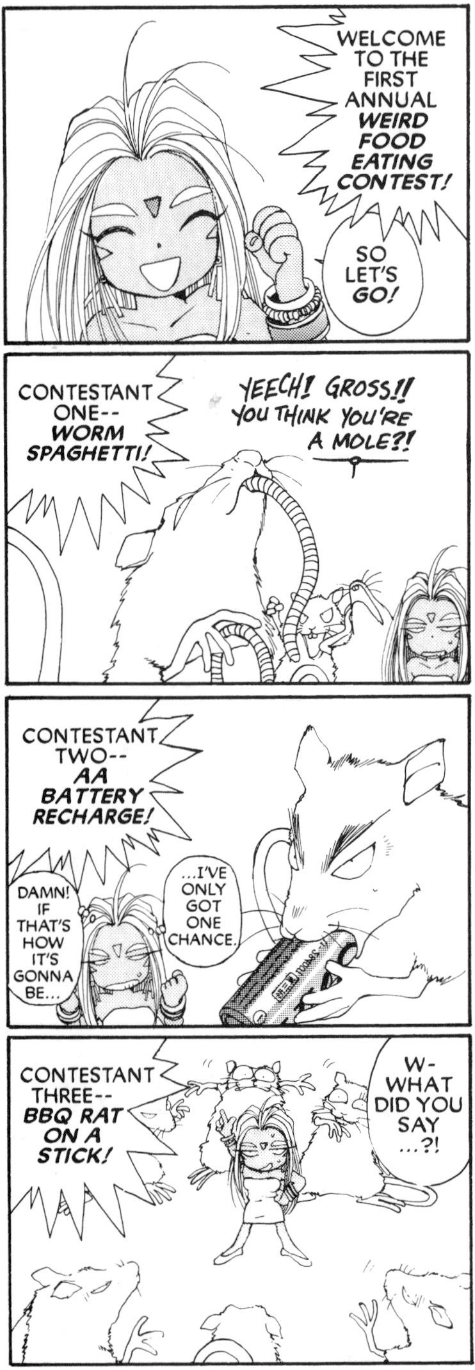
WELCOME TO THE FIRST ANNUAL WEIRD FOOD EATING CONTEST!
SO LET'S GO!
CONTESTANT ONE-- WORM SPAGHETTI!
YEECH! GROSS!! YOU THINK YOU'RE A MOLE?!
CONTESTANT TWO-- AA BATTERY RECHARGE!
DAMN! IF THAT'S HOW IT'S GONNA BE...
...I'VE ONLY GOT ONE CHANCE.
CONTESTANT THREE-- BBQ RAT ON A STICK!
W-WHAT DID YOU SAY ...?!

AMAZING! THE ALL-YOU-CAN-EAT CONTEST!

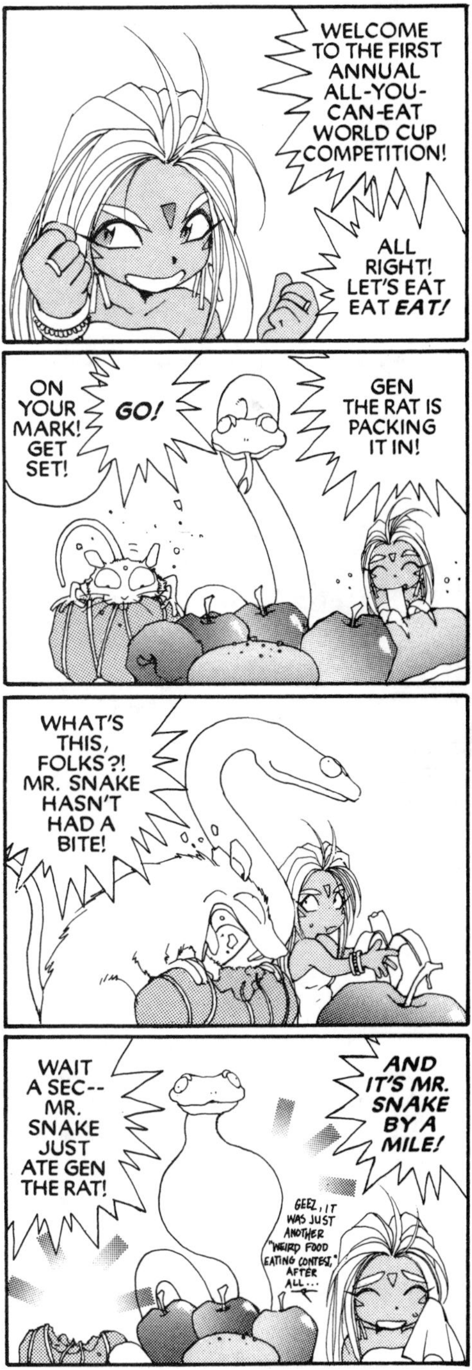
WELCOME TO THE FIRST ANNUAL ALL-YOU-CAN-EAT WORLD CUP COMPETITION!
ALL RIGHT! LET'S EAT EAT *EAT!*
ON YOUR MARK! GET SET!
GO!
GEN THE RAT IS PACKING IT IN!
WHAT'S THIS, FOLKS?! MR. SNAKE HASN'T HAD A BITE!
WAIT A SEC-- MR. SNAKE JUST ATE GEN THE RAT!
AND IT'S MR. SNAKE BY A MILE!
GEEZ, IT WAS JUST ANOTHER "WEIRD FOOD EATING CONTEST," AFTER ALL...

MORISATO, YOU MAY HAVE BREASTS, BUT YOU'RE **STILL** A GUY!
(Might as well dig your grave right now!!)

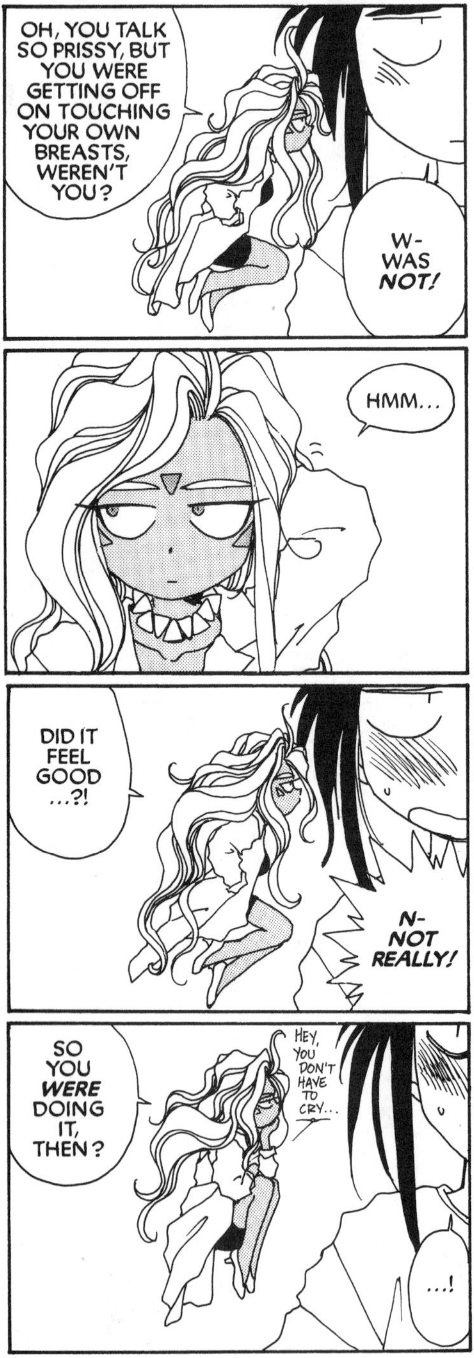
OH, YOU TALK SO PRISSY, BUT YOU WERE GETTING OFF ON TOUCHING YOUR OWN BREASTS, WEREN'T YOU?
W-WAS ***NOT!***
HMM...
DID IT FEEL GOOD ...?!
N-NOT REALLY!
SO YOU ***WERE*** DOING IT, THEN?
HEY, YOU DON'T HAVE TO CRY...
...!

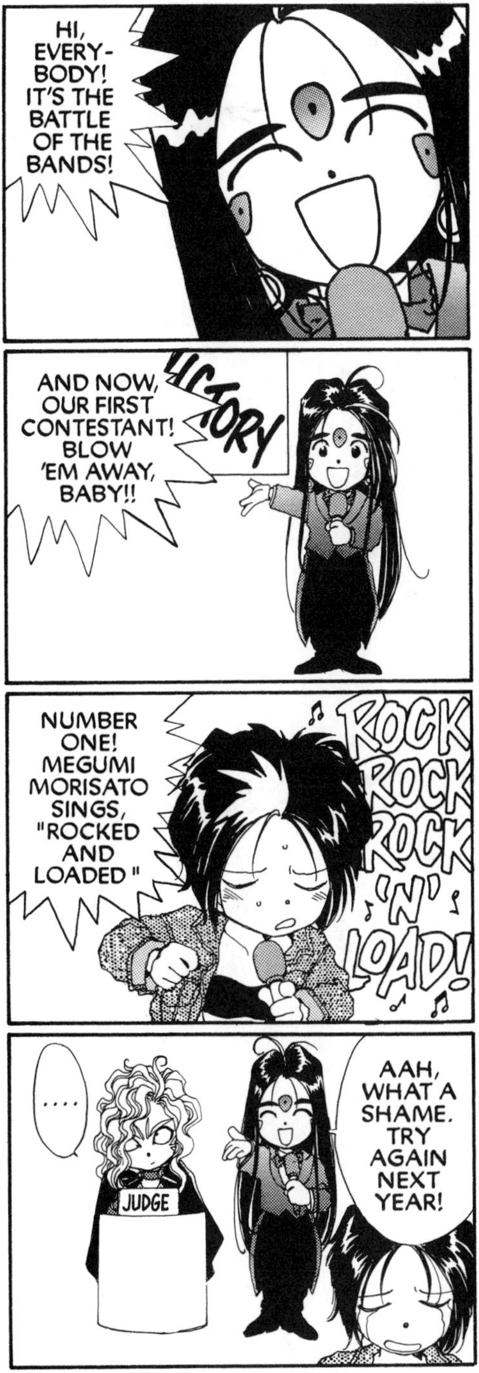
HI, EVERY-BODY! IT'S THE BATTLE OF THE BANDS!
AND NOW, OUR FIRST CONTESTANT! BLOW 'EM AWAY, BABY!!
NUMBER ONE! MEGUMI MORISATO SINGS, "ROCKED AND LOADED"
ROCK ROCK ROCK 'N' LOAD!
....
JUDGE
AAH, WHAT A SHAME. TRY AGAIN NEXT YEAR!

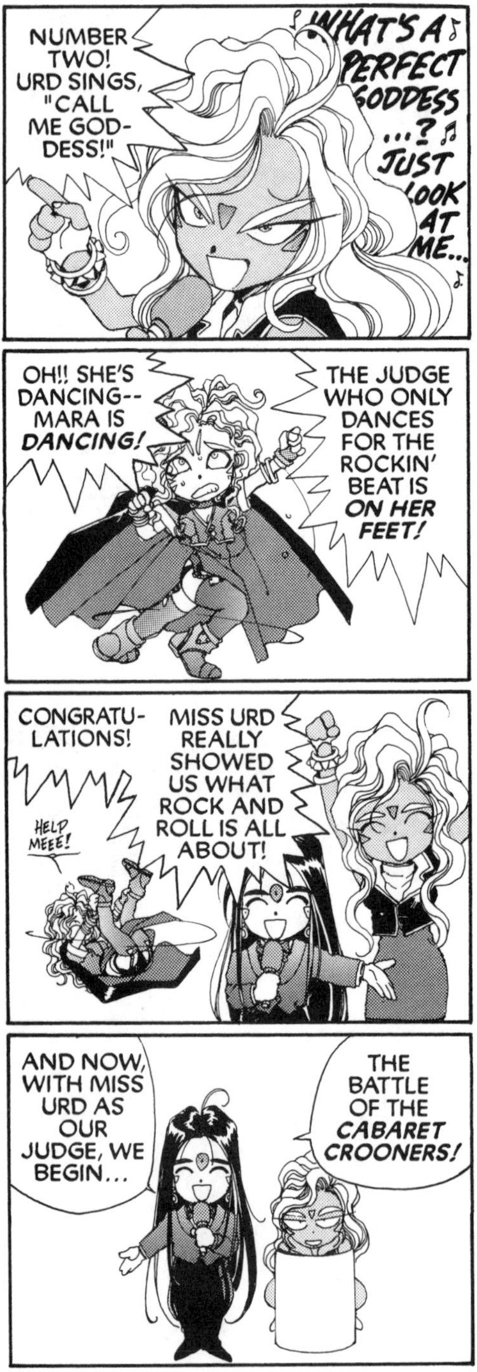
NUMBER TWO! URD SINGS, "CALL ME GOD-DESS!"
WHAT'S A PERFECT GODDESS ...? JUST LOOK AT ME...
OH!! SHE'S DANCING-- MARA IS DANCING!
THE JUDGE WHO ONLY DANCES FOR THE ROCKIN' BEAT IS ON HER FEET!
CONGRATU-LATIONS!
MISS URD REALLY SHOWED US WHAT ROCK AND ROLL IS ALL ABOUT!
HELP MEEE!
AND NOW, WITH MISS URD AS OUR JUDGE, WE BEGIN...
THE BATTLE OF THE CABARET CROONERS!

STORMWRACK - A TALE OF BASEBALL (PART ONE)

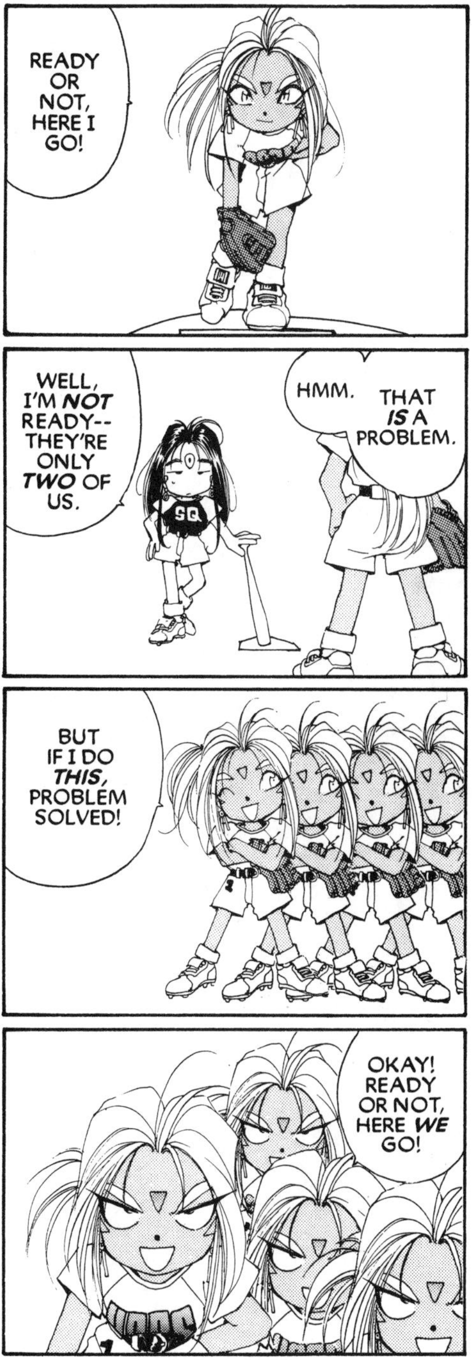
READY OR NOT, HERE I GO!
WELL, I'M *NOT* READY-- THEY'RE ONLY *TWO* OF US.
HMM.
THAT *IS* A PROBLEM.
BUT IF I DO *THIS,* PROBLEM SOLVED!
OKAY! READY OR NOT, HERE *WE* GO!

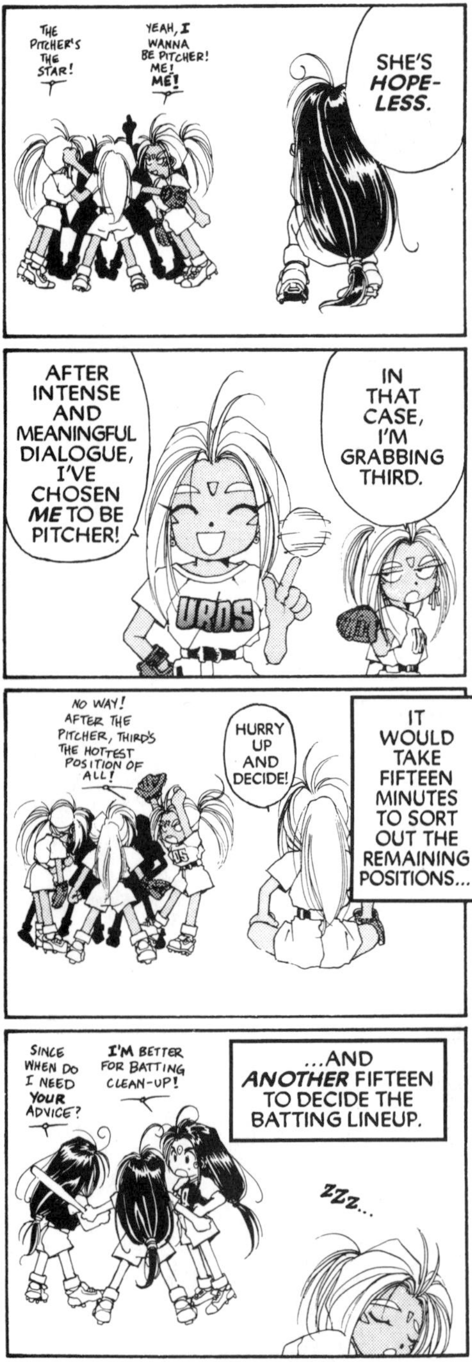

THE PITCHER'S THE STAR!
YEAH, I WANNA BE PITCHER! ME! ME!
SHE'S HOPELESS.
AFTER INTENSE AND MEANINGFUL DIALOGUE, I'VE CHOSEN ME TO BE PITCHER!
IN THAT CASE, I'M GRABBING THIRD.
URDS
NO WAY! AFTER THE PITCHER, THIRD'S THE HOTTEST POSITION OF ALL!
HURRY UP AND DECIDE!
IT WOULD TAKE FIFTEEN MINUTES TO SORT OUT THE REMAINING POSITIONS...
SINCE WHEN DO I NEED YOUR ADVICE?
I'M BETTER FOR BATTING CLEAN-UP!
...AND ANOTHER FIFTEEN TO DECIDE THE BATTING LINEUP.
ZZZ...

STORMWRACK
PART THE SECOND

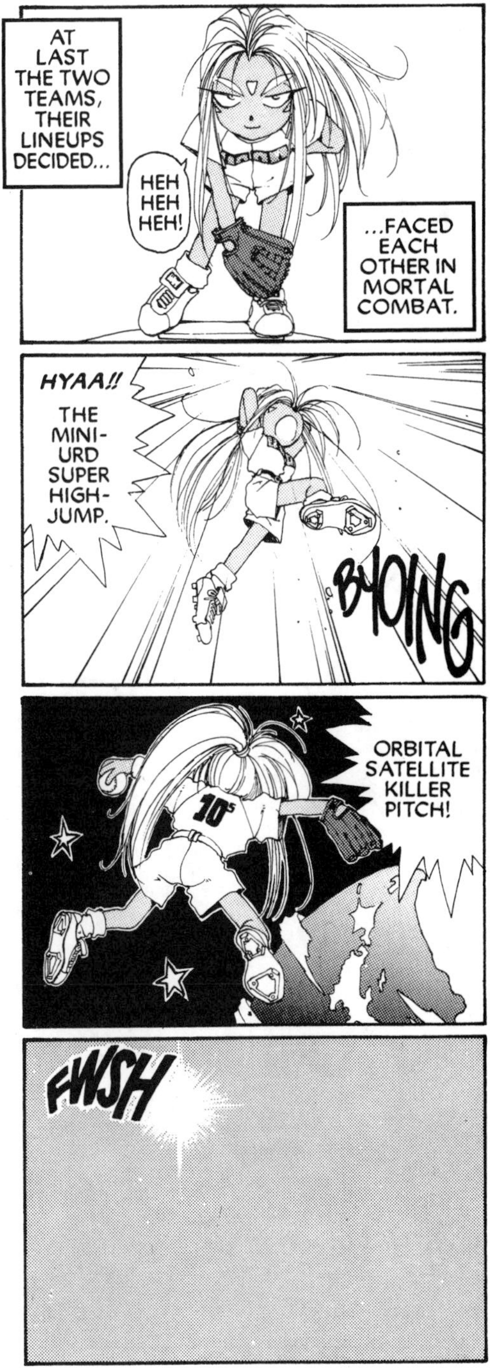
AT LAST THE TWO TEAMS, THEIR LINEUPS DECIDED...
HEH HEH HEH!
...FACED EACH OTHER IN MORTAL COMBAT.
HYAA!!
THE MINI-URD SUPER HIGH-JUMP.
BYOING
ORBITAL SATELLITE KILLER PITCH!
10
FWSH

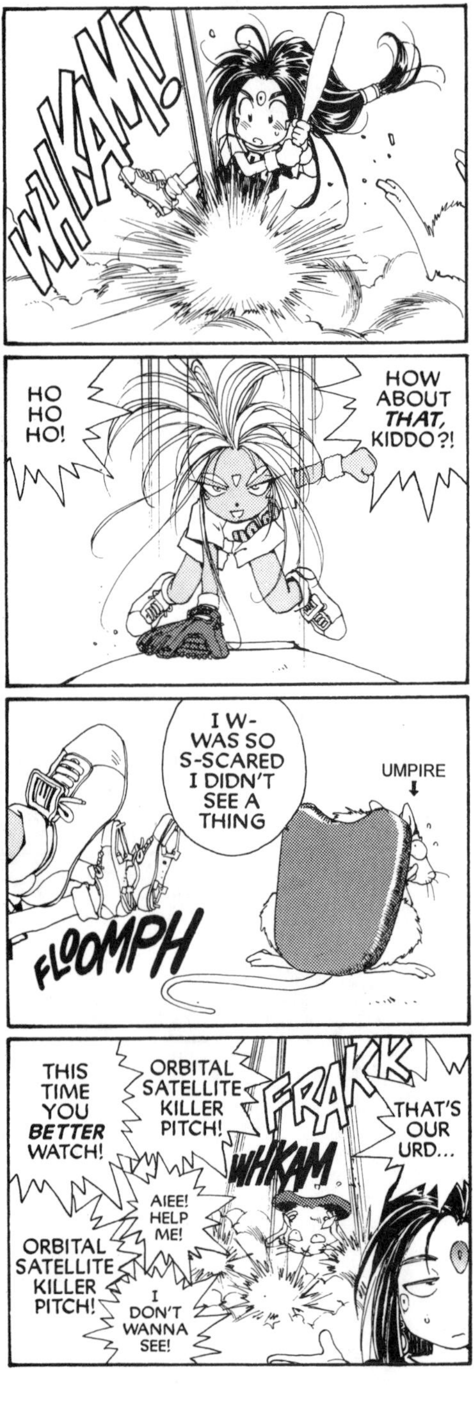
WHKAM!
HO HO HO!
HOW ABOUT *THAT*, KIDDO?!
I W-WAS SO S-SCARED I DIDN'T SEE A THING
UMPIRE
FLOOMPH
THIS TIME YOU *BETTER* WATCH!
ORBITAL SATELLITE KILLER PITCH!
FRAKK
THAT'S OUR URD...
WHKAM
AIEE! HELP ME!
ORBITAL SATELLITE KILLER PITCH!
I DON'T WANNA SEE!

STORMWRACK PART THE THIRD

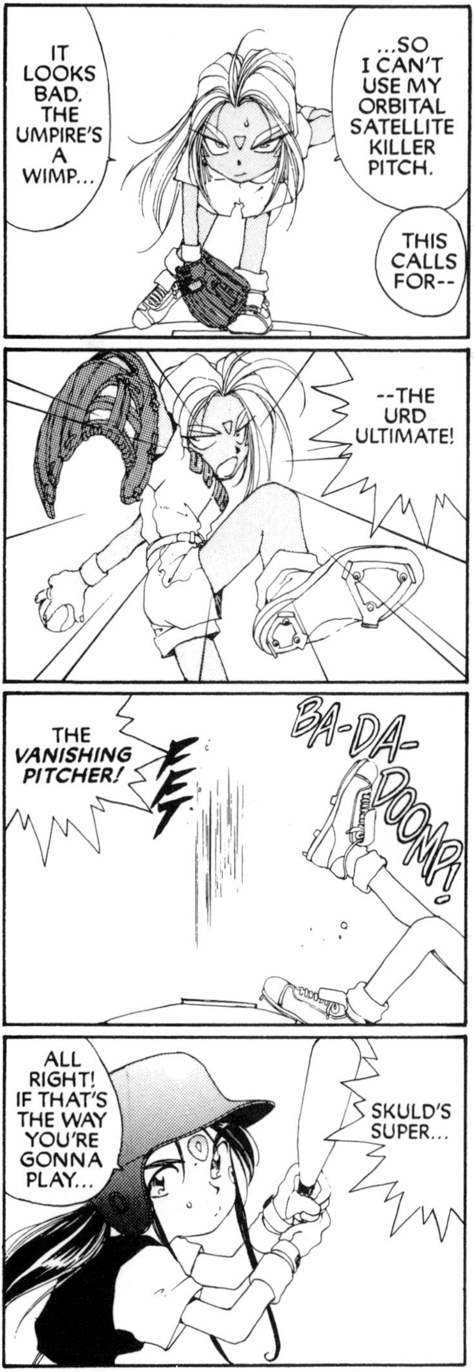
IT LOOKS BAD. THE UMPIRE'S A WIMP...
...SO I CAN'T USE MY ORBITAL SATELLITE KILLER PITCH.
THIS CALLS FOR--
--THE URD ULTIMATE!
THE *VANISHING PITCHER!*
BA-DA-DOOMP!
ALL RIGHT! IF THAT'S THE WAY YOU'RE GONNA PLAY...
SKULD'S SUPER...

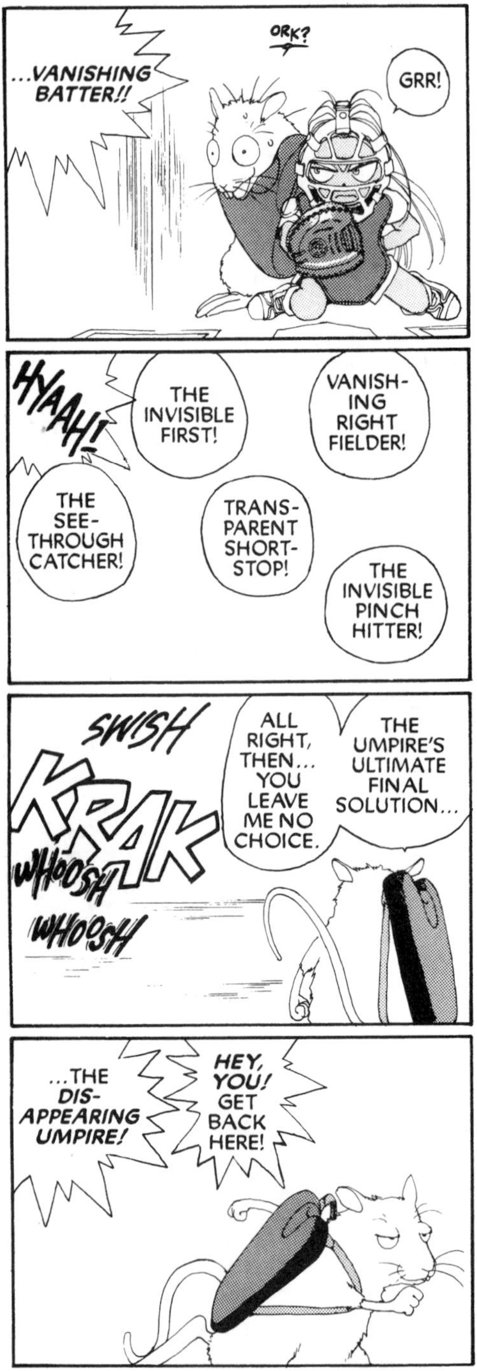
...VANISHING BATTER!!
ORK?
GRR!
HYAAAH!
THE INVISIBLE FIRST!
VANISH-ING RIGHT FIELDER!
THE SEE-THROUGH CATCHER!
TRANS-PARENT SHORT-STOP!
THE INVISIBLE PINCH HITTER!
SWISH
KRAK
WHOOSH
WHOOSH
ALL RIGHT, THEN... YOU LEAVE ME NO CHOICE.
THE UMPIRE'S ULTIMATE FINAL SOLUTION...
...THE DIS-APPEARING UMPIRE!
HEY, YOU! GET BACK HERE!

STORMWRACK
A TALE OF BASEBALL
THE SIDE STORY

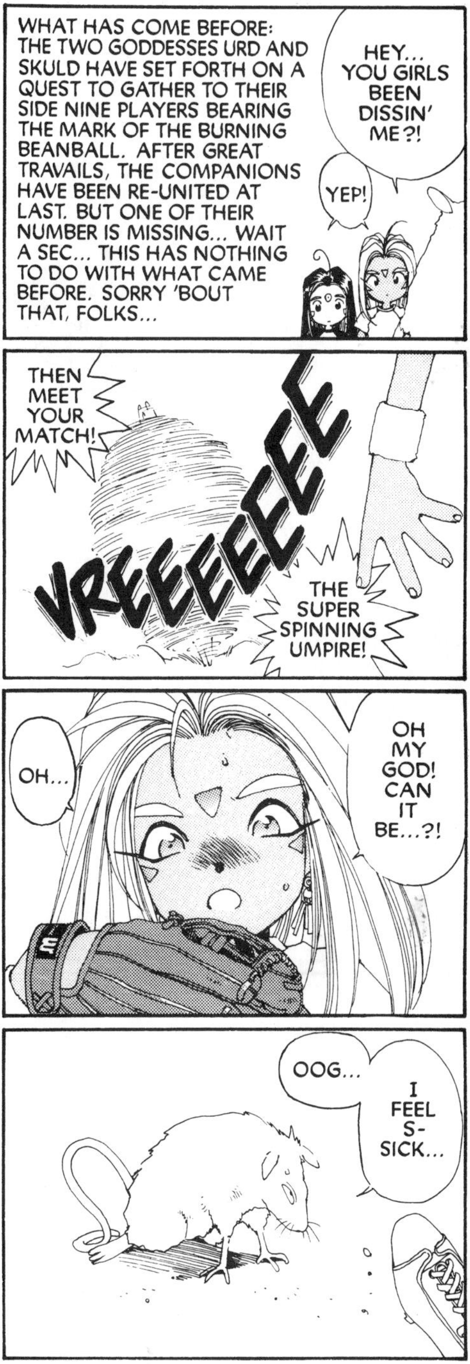
WHAT HAS COME BEFORE: THE TWO GODDESSES URD AND SKULD HAVE SET FORTH ON A QUEST TO GATHER TO THEIR SIDE NINE PLAYERS BEARING THE MARK OF THE BURNING BEANBALL. AFTER GREAT TRAVAILS, THE COMPANIONS HAVE BEEN RE-UNITED AT LAST. BUT ONE OF THEIR NUMBER IS MISSING... WAIT A SEC... THIS HAS NOTHING TO DO WITH WHAT CAME BEFORE. SORRY 'BOUT THAT, FOLKS...
HEY... YOU GIRLS BEEN DISSIN' ME?!
YEP!
THEN MEET YOUR MATCH!
VREEEEEEEEEE
THE SUPER SPINNING UMPIRE!
OH...
OH MY GOD! CAN IT BE...?!
OOG...
I FEEL S-SICK...

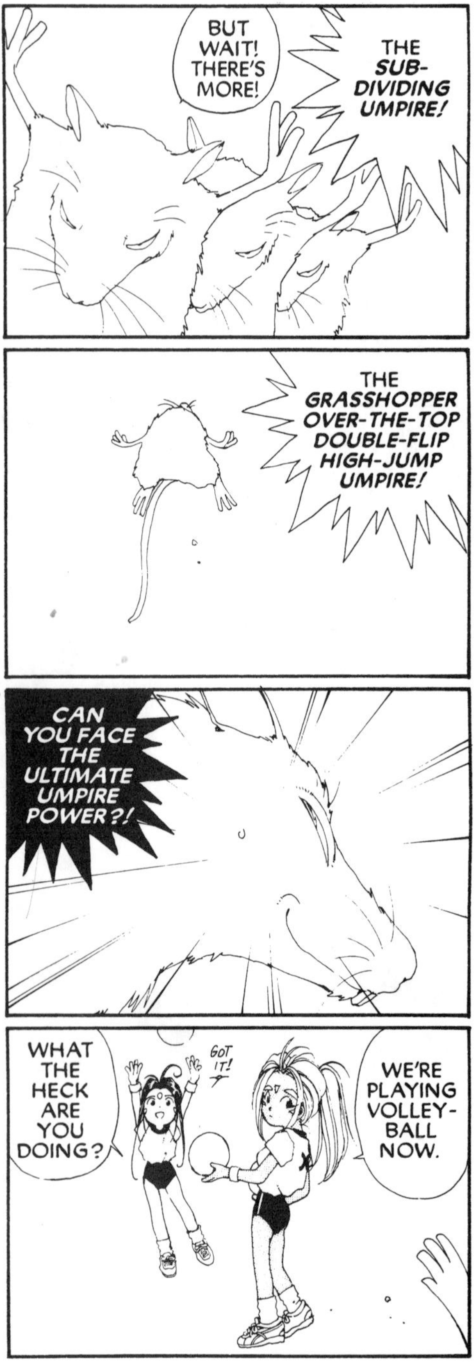
BUT WAIT! THERE'S MORE!
THE *SUB-DIVIDING UMPIRE!*
THE *GRASSHOPPER OVER-THE-TOP DOUBLE-FLIP HIGH-JUMP UMPIRE!*
CAN YOU FACE THE ULTIMATE UMPIRE POWER?!
WHAT THE HECK ARE YOU DOING?
GOT IT!
WE'RE PLAYING VOLLEY-BALL NOW.

◆ FORWARD TO THE FUTURE! ◆

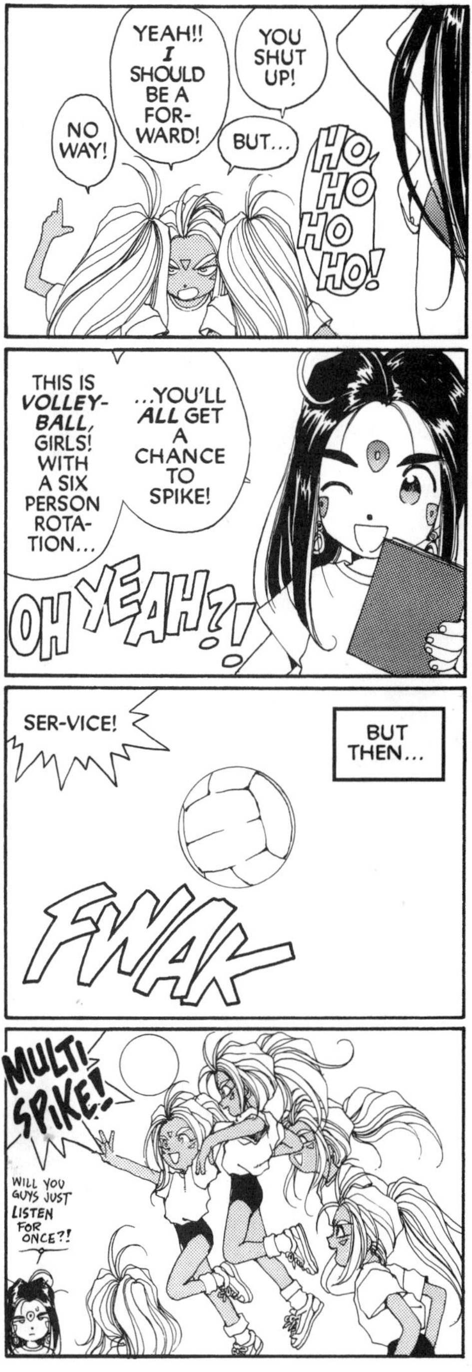
YEAH!! *I* SHOULD BE A FOR-WARD!
NO WAY!
YOU SHUT UP!
BUT...
HO HO HO HO HO!
THIS IS *VOLLEY-BALL*, GIRLS! WITH A SIX PERSON ROTA-TION...
...YOU'LL *ALL* GET A CHANCE TO SPIKE!
OH YEAH?!
SER-VICE!
BUT THEN...
FWAK
MULTI SPIKE!
WILL YOU GUYS JUST LISTEN FOR ONCE?!

HOLE-IN-ONE GYM SHORTS

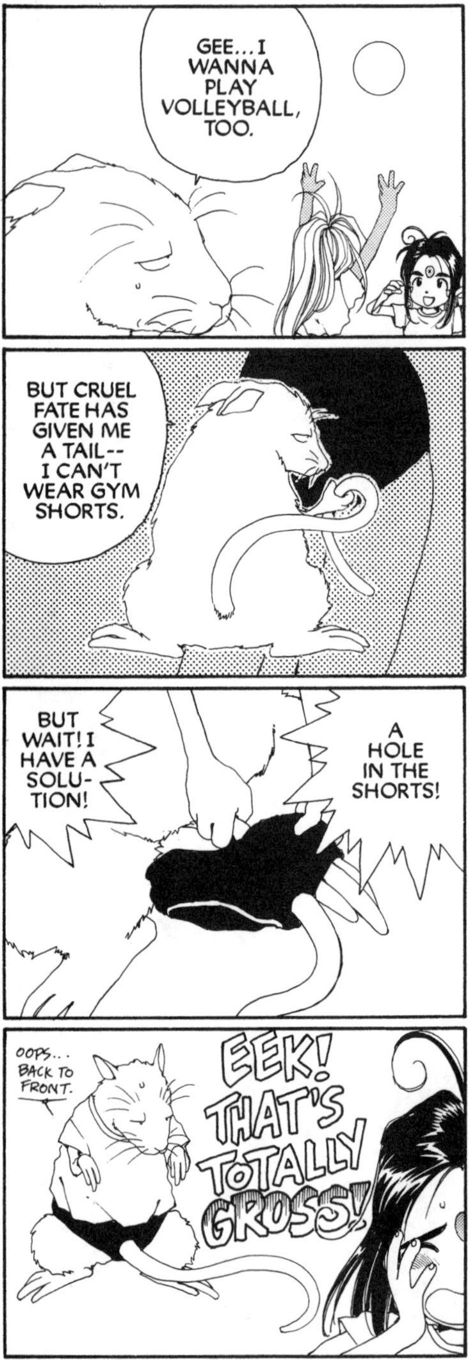
GEE...I WANNA PLAY VOLLEYBALL, TOO.
BUT CRUEL FATE HAS GIVEN ME A TAIL-- I CAN'T WEAR GYM SHORTS.
BUT WAIT! I HAVE A SOLU-TION!
A HOLE IN THE SHORTS!
OOPS... BACK TO FRONT.
EEK! THAT'S TOTALLY GROSS!

◆ SUPER SPIKE! ◆

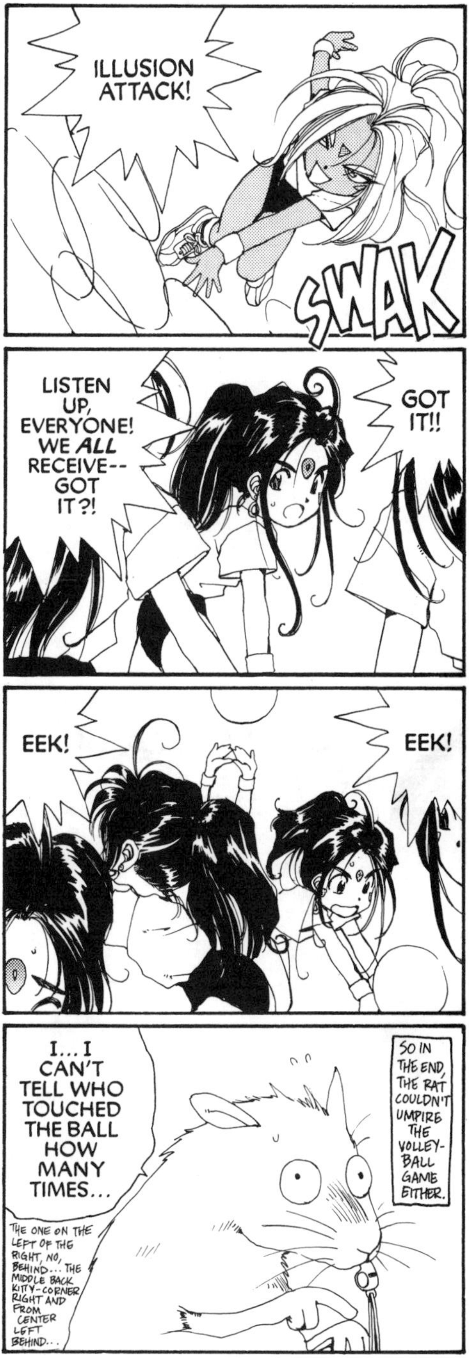
ILLUSION ATTACK!
SWAK
LISTEN UP, EVERYONE! WE ALL RECEIVE-- GOT IT?!
GOT IT!!
EEK!
EEK!
I... I CAN'T TELL WHO TOUCHED THE BALL HOW MANY TIMES...
THE ONE ON THE LEFT OF THE RIGHT, NO, BEHIND... THE MIDDLE BACK KITTY-CORNER RIGHT AND FROM CENTER LEFT BEHIND...
SO IN THE END, THE RAT COULDN'T UMPIRE THE VOLLEY-BALL GAME EITHER.

ATTACKING FURIES

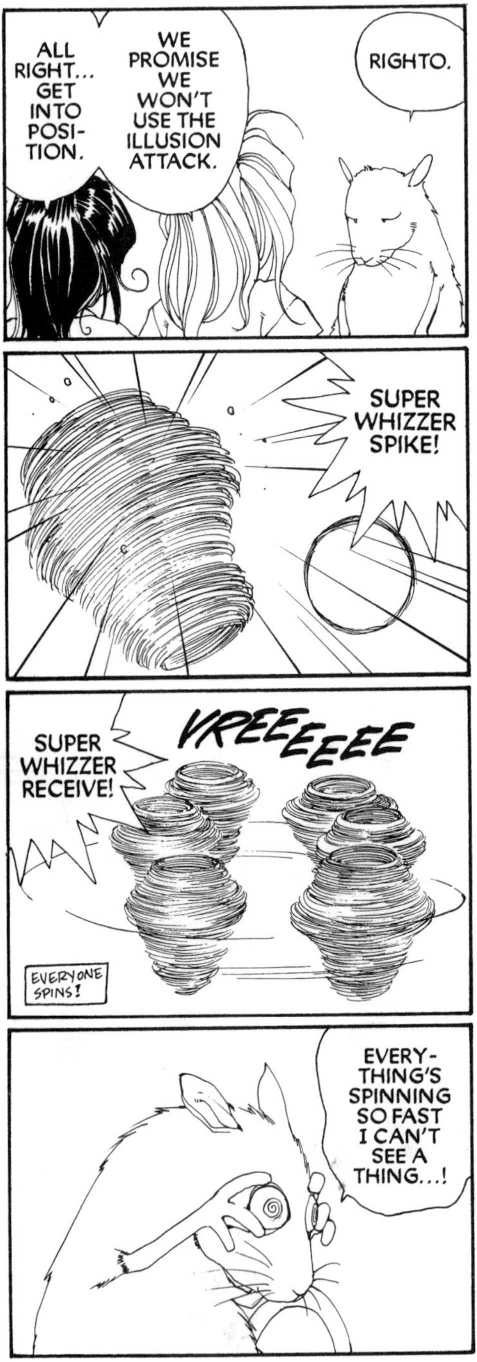

ALL RIGHT… GET INTO POSI-TION.
WE PROMISE WE WON'T USE THE ILLUSION ATTACK.
RIGHTO.
SUPER WHIZZER SPIKE!
SUPER WHIZZER RECEIVE!
VREEEEEEE
EVERYONE SPINS!
EVERY-THING'S SPINNING SO FAST I CAN'T SEE A THING…!

◆ IT HAS ITS ADVANTAGES ◆

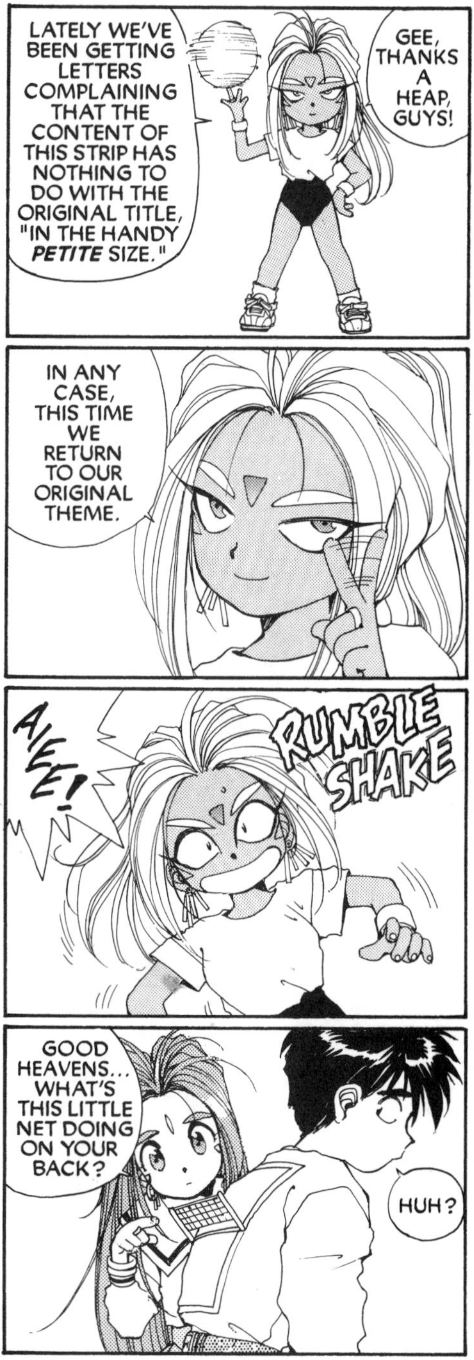
LATELY WE'VE BEEN GETTING LETTERS COMPLAINING THAT THE CONTENT OF THIS STRIP HAS NOTHING TO DO WITH THE ORIGINAL TITLE, "IN THE HANDY *PETITE* SIZE."
GEE, THANKS A HEAP, GUYS!
IN ANY CASE, THIS TIME WE RETURN TO OUR ORIGINAL THEME.
AIEEE!
RUMBLE SHAKE
GOOD HEAVENS... WHAT'S THIS LITTLE NET DOING ON YOUR BACK?
HUH?

A STAR IS BORN— THE COMING OF URD

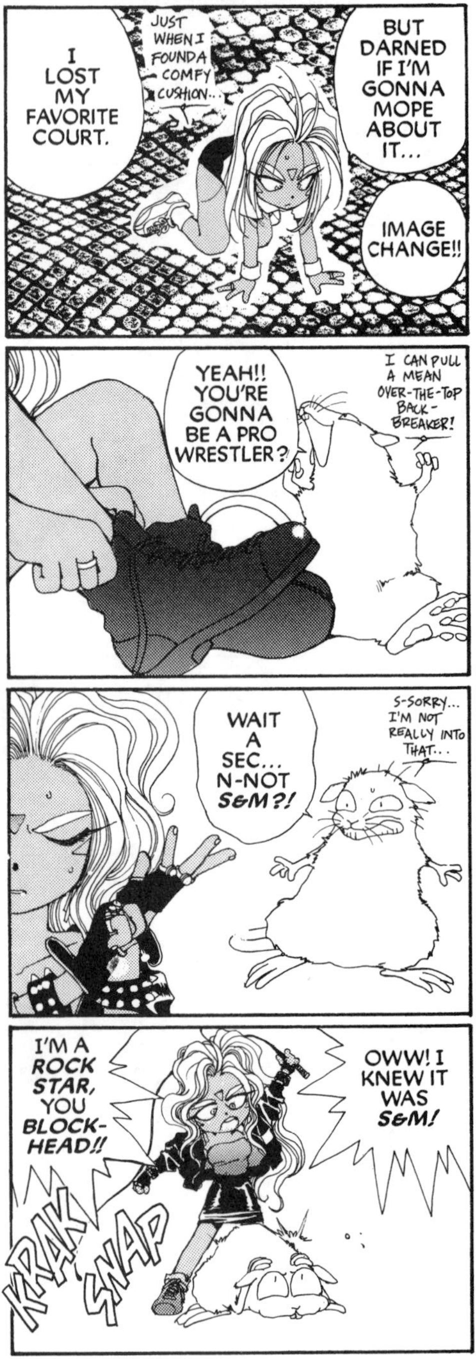
I LOST MY FAVORITE COURT.
JUST WHEN I FOUND A COMFY CUSHION...
BUT DARNED IF I'M GONNA MOPE ABOUT IT...
IMAGE CHANGE!!
YEAH!! YOU'RE GONNA BE A PRO WRESTLER?
I CAN PULL A MEAN OVER-THE-TOP BACK-BREAKER!
WAIT A SEC... N-NOT S&M?!
S-SORRY... I'M NOT REALLY INTO THAT...
I'M A ROCK STAR, YOU BLOCK-HEAD!!
OWW! I KNEW IT WAS S&M!
KRAK
SNAP

OH MY CARTOONIST! (Special Road Trip Edition)
Kikuko Inogashira (pseudonym): Belldandy's voice actress

"BATTLE! The Challenge of the Fake Food Samples!" (an almost-true story)

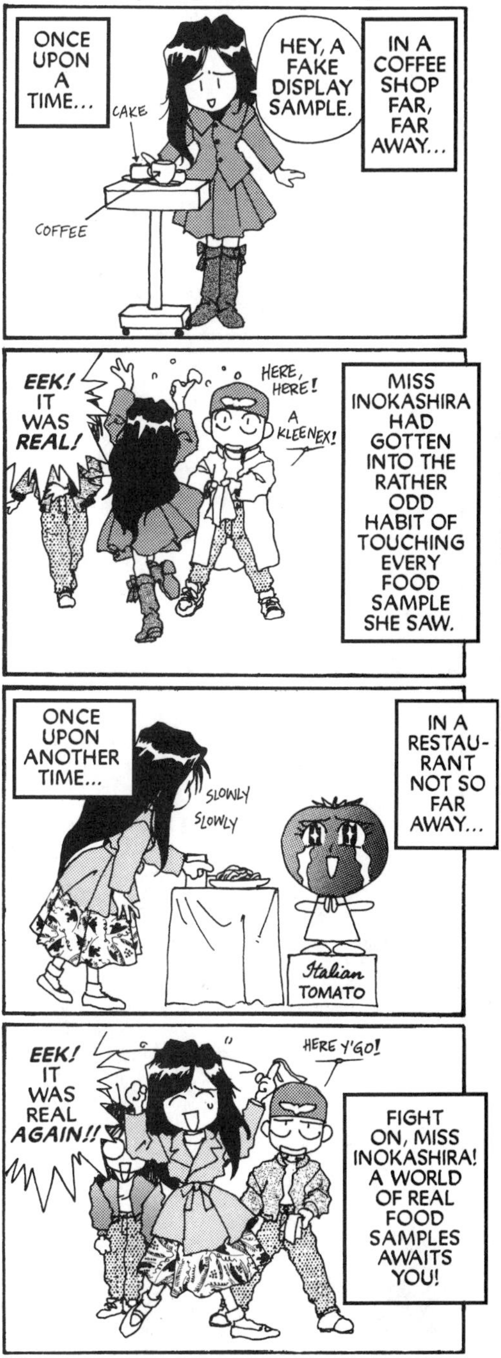
ONCE UPON A TIME...
CAKE
COFFEE
HEY, A FAKE DISPLAY SAMPLE.
IN A COFFEE SHOP FAR, FAR AWAY...
EEK! IT WAS REAL!
HERE, HERE!
A KLEENEX!
MISS INOKASHIRA HAD GOTTEN INTO THE RATHER ODD HABIT OF TOUCHING EVERY FOOD SAMPLE SHE SAW.
ONCE UPON ANOTHER TIME...
SLOWLY
SLOWLY
IN A RESTAU-RANT NOT SO FAR AWAY...
Italian TOMATO
EEK! IT WAS REAL AGAIN!!
HERE Y'GO!
FIGHT ON, MISS INOKASHIRA! A WORLD OF REAL FOOD SAMPLES AWAITS YOU!

▲ ANY SIMILARITY WITH ANY PERSON LIVING OR DEAD IS PURELY COINCIDENTAL. HONEST! I SWEAR!

◆ IS THE MISO SOUP IN YOUR HOUSE SAFE? ◆

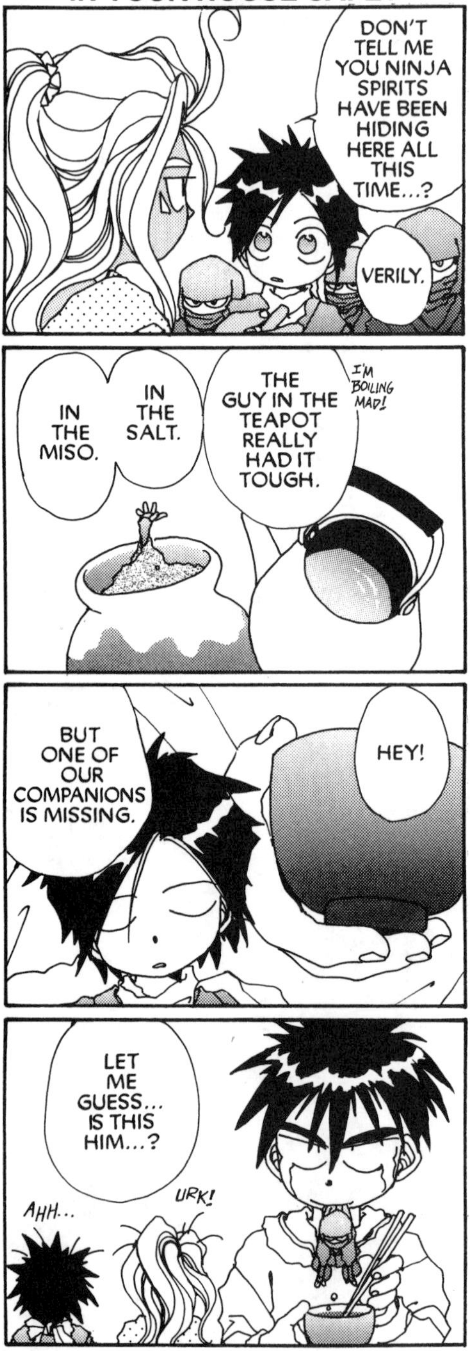
DON'T TELL ME YOU NINJA SPIRITS HAVE BEEN HIDING HERE ALL THIS TIME...?
VERILY.
IN THE MISO.
IN THE SALT.
THE GUY IN THE TEAPOT REALLY HAD IT TOUGH.
I'M BOILING MAD!
BUT ONE OF OUR COMPANIONS IS MISSING.
HEY!
LET ME GUESS... IS THIS HIM...?
AHH...
URK!

WARNING: EXCESSIVE SUB-DIVISION CAN BE HAZARDOUS TO YOUR HEALTH

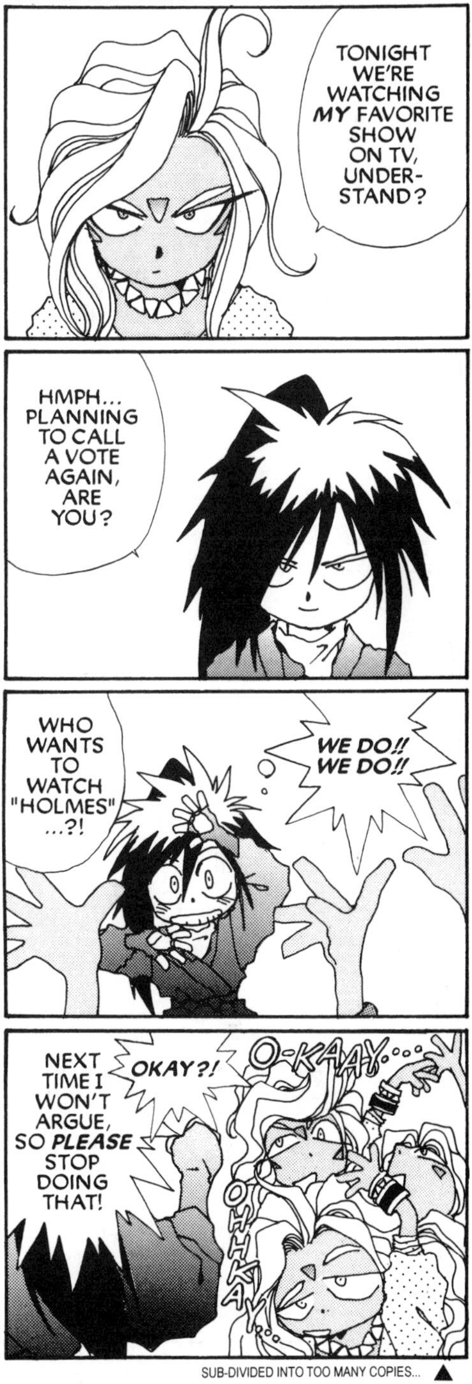
TONIGHT WE'RE WATCHING *MY* FAVORITE SHOW ON TV, UNDER-STAND?
HMPH... PLANNING TO CALL A VOTE AGAIN, ARE YOU?
WHO WANTS TO WATCH "HOLMES" ...?!
WE DO!! WE DO!!
NEXT TIME I WON'T ARGUE, SO *PLEASE* STOP DOING THAT!
OKAY?!
O-KAAAY...
OHHKAY...

SUB-DIVIDED INTO TOO MANY COPIES... ▲

A NINJA'S LOT IS NOT A HAPPY ONE

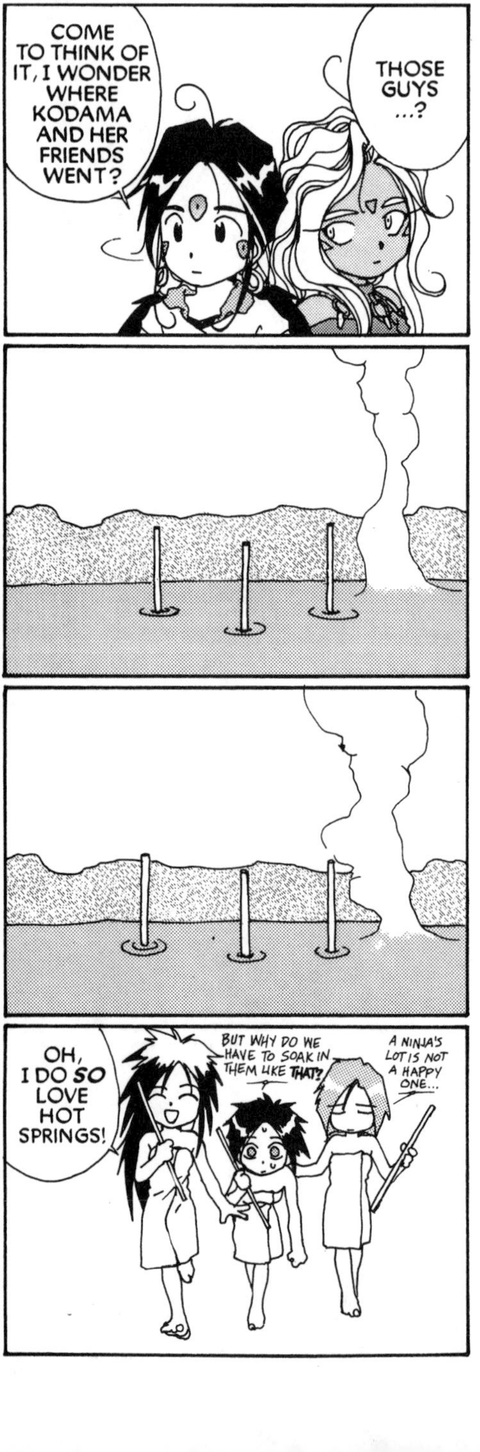
COME TO THINK OF IT, I WONDER WHERE KODAMA AND HER FRIENDS WENT?
THOSE GUYS ...?
OH, I DO SO LOVE HOT SPRINGS!
BUT WHY DO WE HAVE TO SOAK IN THEM LIKE THAT?
A NINJA'S LOT IS NOT A HAPPY ONE...

A NINJA'S LOT IS *DEFINITELY* NOT A HAPPY ONE

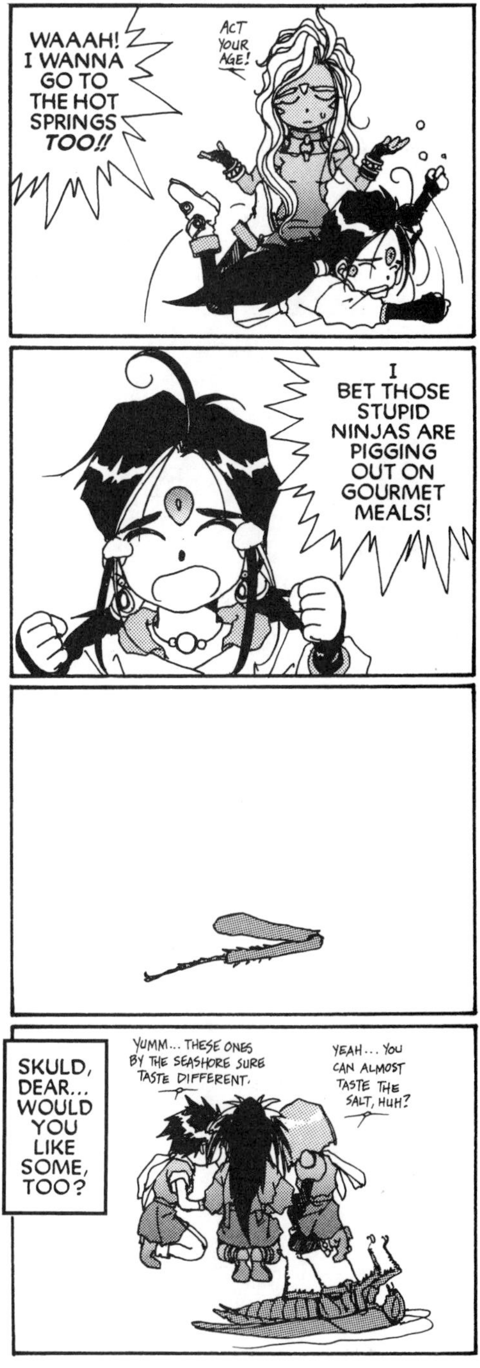
WAAAH! I WANNA GO TO THE HOT SPRINGS *TOO!!*
ACT YOUR AGE!
I BET THOSE STUPID NINJAS ARE PIGGING OUT ON GOURMET MEALS!
SKULD, DEAR... WOULD YOU LIKE SOME, TOO?
YUMM... THESE ONES BY THE SEASHORE SURE TASTE DIFFERENT.
YEAH... YOU CAN ALMOST TASTE THE SALT, HUH?

URD OF THE SHINING TRIANGLE

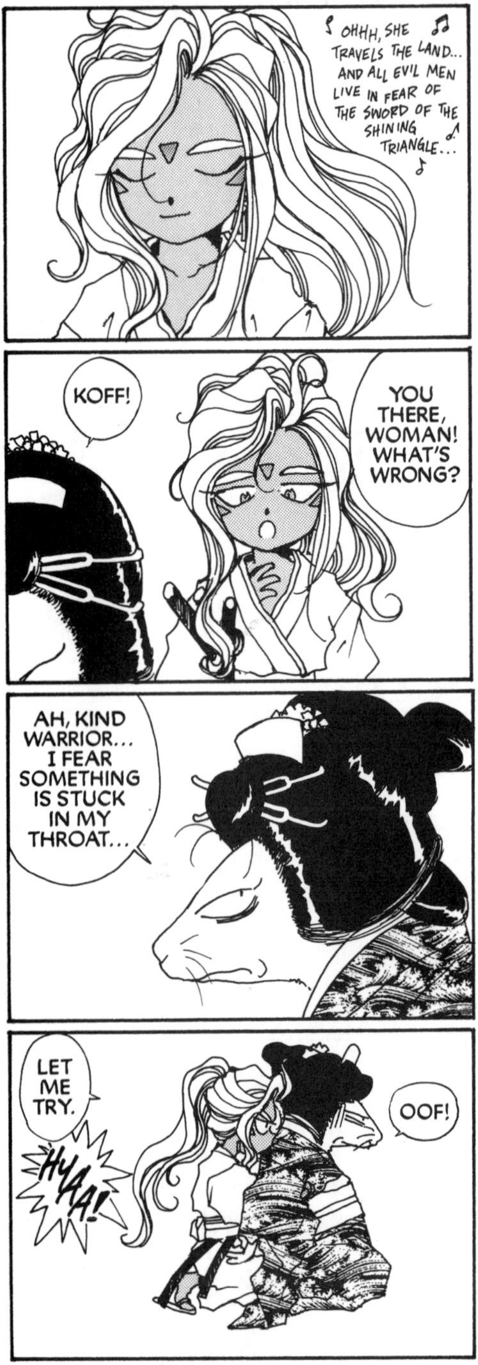

OHHH, SHE TRAVELS THE LAND... AND ALL EVIL MEN LIVE IN FEAR OF THE SWORD OF THE SHINING TRIANGLE...
KOFF!
YOU THERE, WOMAN! WHAT'S WRONG?
AH, KIND WARRIOR... I FEAR SOMETHING IS STUCK IN MY THROAT...
LET ME TRY.
HYAA!
OOF!

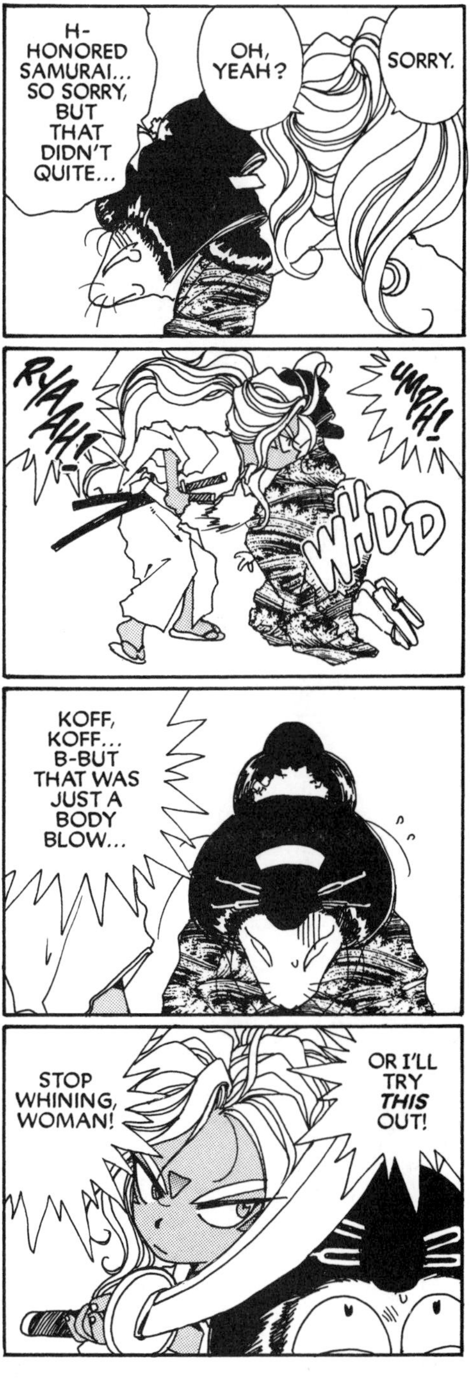
H-HONORED SAMURAI... SO SORRY, BUT THAT DIDN'T QUITE...
OH, YEAH?
SORRY.
RYAAAH!
UMPH!
WHDD
KOFF, KOFF... B-BUT THAT WAS JUST A BODY BLOW...
STOP WHINING, WOMAN!
OR I'LL TRY *THIS* OUT!

WE'VE PUT THE BAND ON HOLD

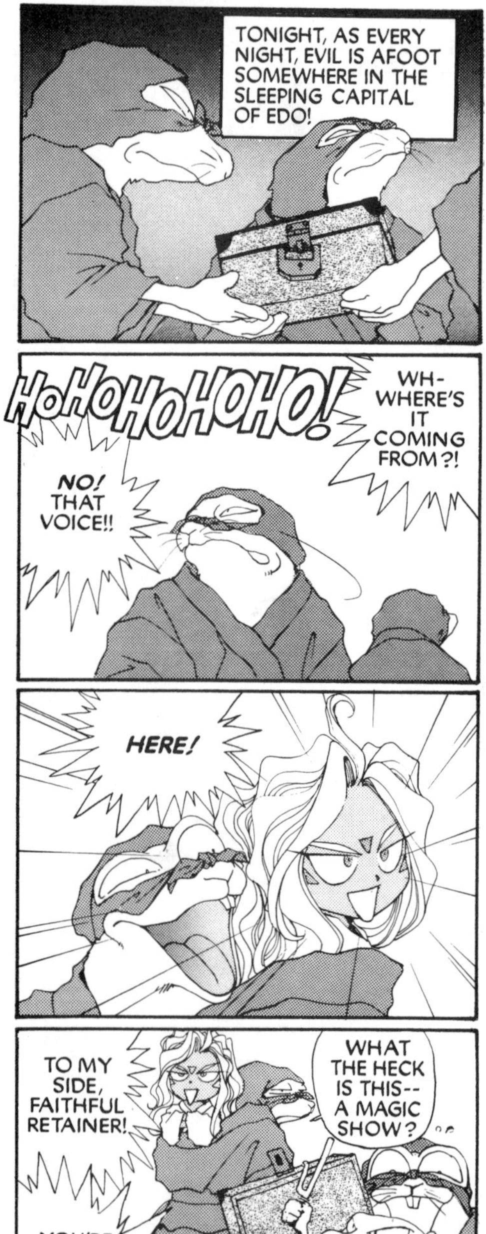
TONIGHT, AS EVERY NIGHT, EVIL IS AFOOT SOMEWHERE IN THE SLEEPING CAPITAL OF EDO!
HOHOHOHOHOHO!
WH-WHERE'S IT COMING FROM?!
NO! THAT VOICE!!
HERE!
TO MY SIDE, FAITHFUL RETAINER!
WHAT THE HECK IS THIS-- A MAGIC SHOW?
YOU'RE UNDER ARREST, VILE MISCREANTS!

LITTLE GAN, THE FAITHFUL RAT-AINER

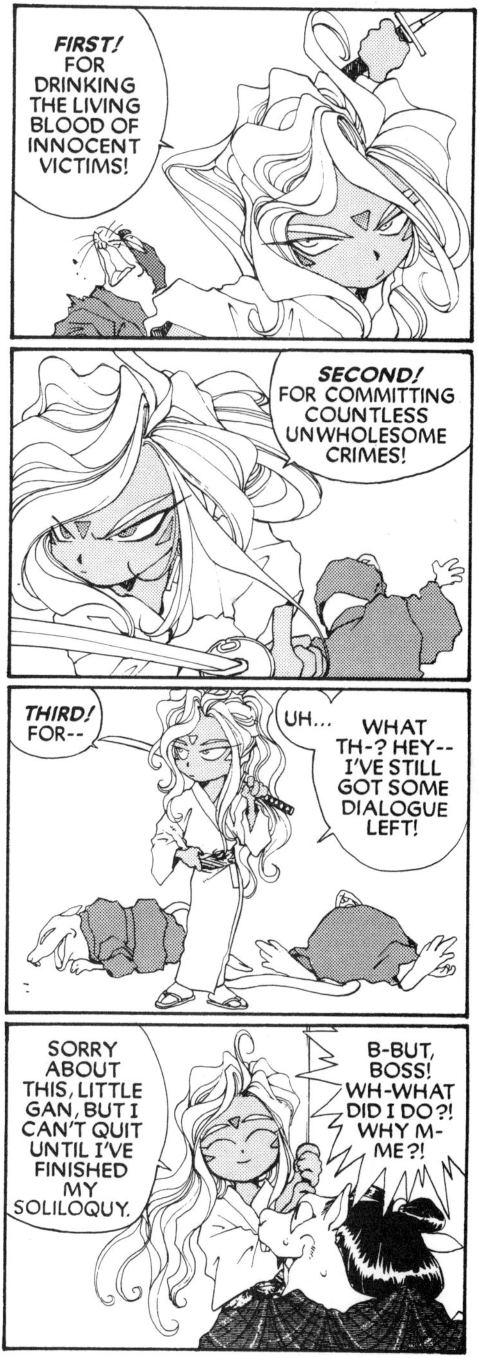

FIRST! FOR DRINKING THE LIVING BLOOD OF INNOCENT VICTIMS!
SECOND! FOR COMMITTING COUNTLESS UNWHOLESOME CRIMES!
THIRD! FOR--
UH...
WHAT TH-? HEY-- I'VE STILL GOT SOME DIALOGUE LEFT!
SORRY ABOUT THIS, LITTLE GAN, BUT I CAN'T QUIT UNTIL I'VE FINISHED MY SOLILOQUY.
B-BUT, BOSS! WH-WHAT DID I DO?! WHY M-ME?!

◆LET'S START A BAND!◆

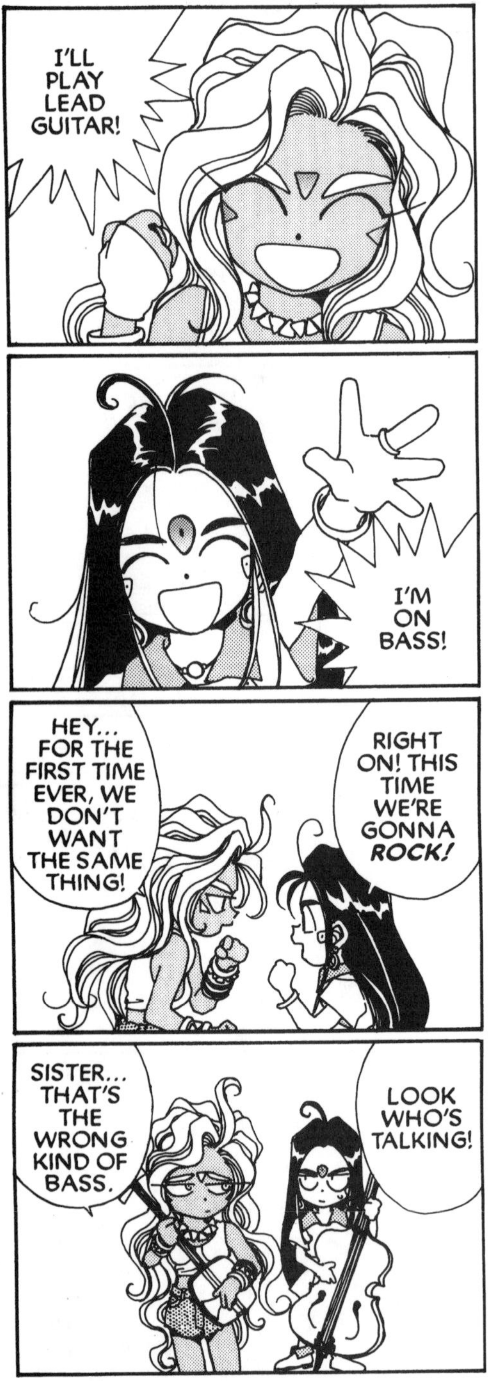
I'LL PLAY LEAD GUITAR!
I'M ON BASS!
HEY... FOR THE FIRST TIME EVER, WE DON'T WANT THE SAME THING!
RIGHT ON! THIS TIME WE'RE GONNA *ROCK!*
SISTER... THAT'S THE WRONG KIND OF BASS.
LOOK WHO'S TALKING!

SEARCHING FOR MISTER GOOD-DRUMMER

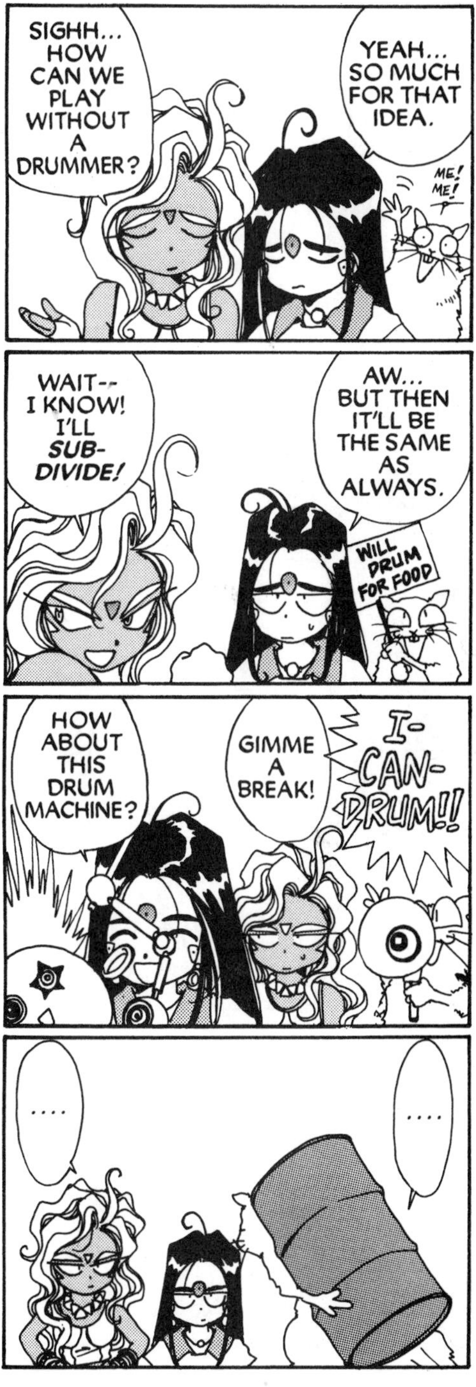
SIGHH... HOW CAN WE PLAY WITHOUT A DRUMMER?
YEAH... SO MUCH FOR THAT IDEA.
ME! ME!
WAIT-- I KNOW! I'LL *SUB-DIVIDE!*
AW... BUT THEN IT'LL BE THE SAME AS ALWAYS.
WILL DRUM FOR FOOD
HOW ABOUT THIS DRUM MACHINE?
GIMME A BREAK!
I-CAN-DRUM!!
....
....

YOU TOO CAN PLAY DRUMS!

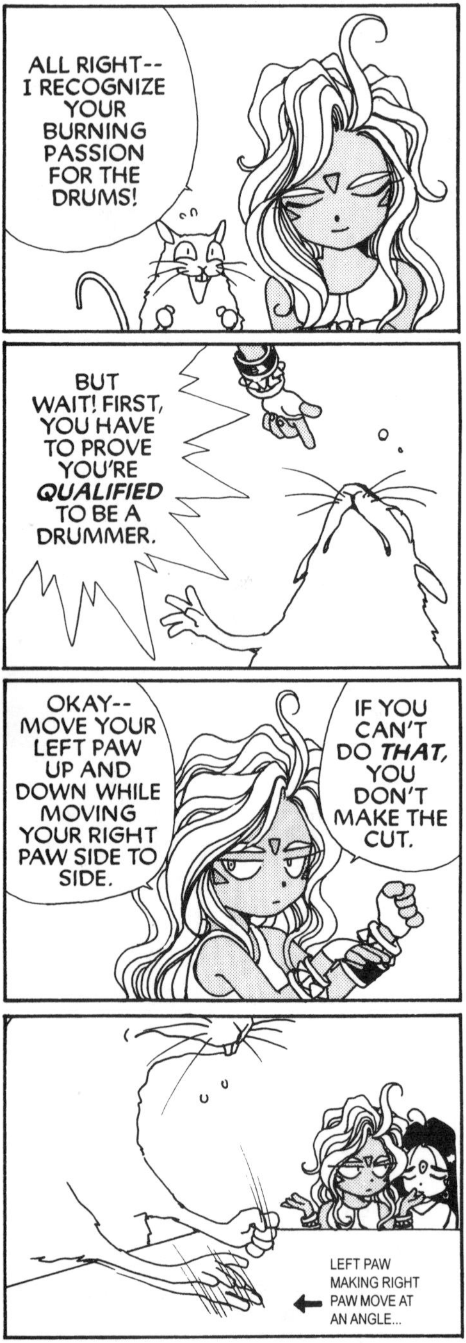
ALL RIGHT-- I RECOGNIZE YOUR BURNING PASSION FOR THE DRUMS!
BUT WAIT! FIRST, YOU HAVE TO PROVE YOU'RE *QUALIFIED* TO BE A DRUMMER.
OKAY-- MOVE YOUR LEFT PAW UP AND DOWN WHILE MOVING YOUR RIGHT PAW SIDE TO SIDE.
IF YOU CAN'T DO *THAT,* YOU DON'T MAKE THE CUT.
LEFT PAW MAKING RIGHT PAW MOVE AT AN ANGLE...

(MAYBE, MAYBE NOT...)

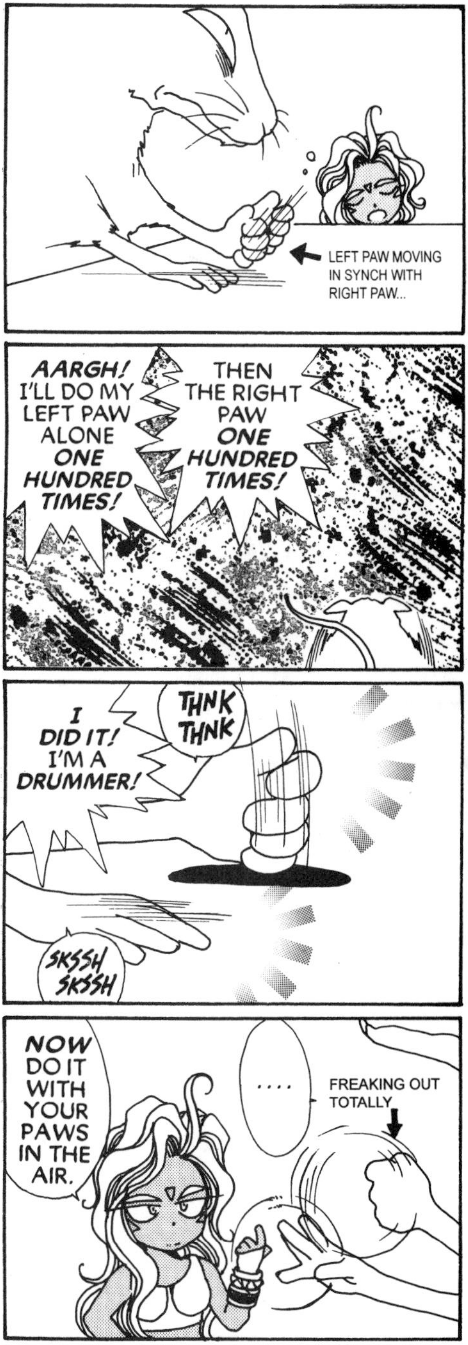
LEFT PAW MOVING IN SYNCH WITH RIGHT PAW...
AARGH! I'LL DO MY LEFT PAW ALONE ONE HUNDRED TIMES!
THEN THE RIGHT PAW ONE HUNDRED TIMES!
I DID IT! I'M A DRUMMER!
THNK THNK
SKSSH SKSSH
NOW DO IT WITH YOUR PAWS IN THE AIR.
....
FREAKING OUT TOTALLY

SPECIAL TRAINING: OBSERVATIONS ON PRACTICAL TECHNIQUE

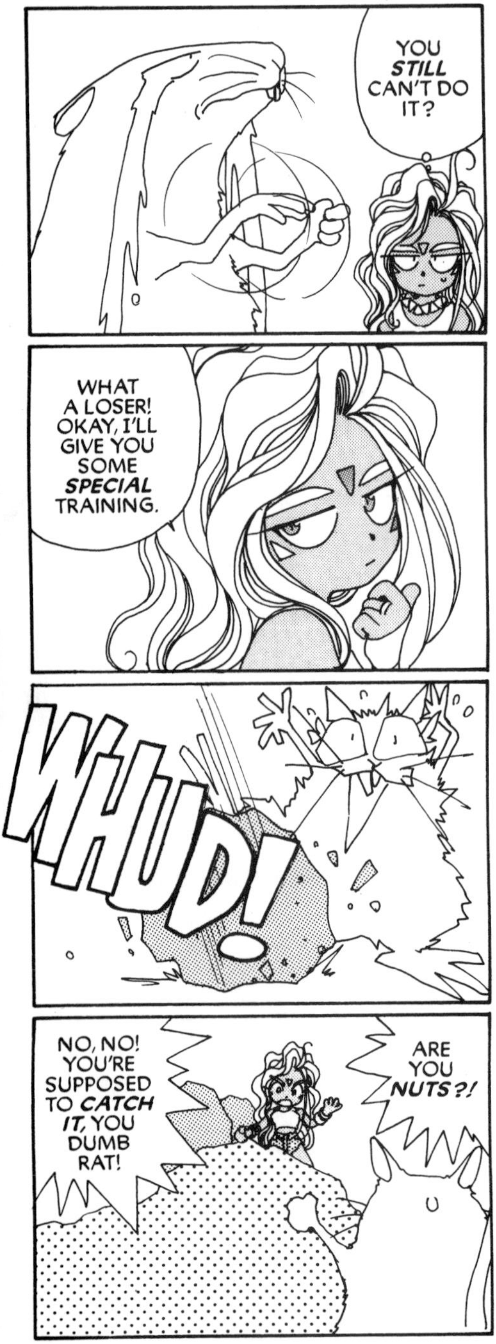
YOU *STILL* CAN'T DO IT?
WHAT A LOSER! OKAY, I'LL GIVE YOU SOME *SPECIAL* TRAINING.
WHUD!
NO, NO! YOU'RE SUPPOSED TO *CATCH IT,* YOU DUMB RAT!
ARE YOU *NUTS?!*

SPECIAL TRAINING VERSUS RESULTS: A STUDY IN NON-CAUSALITY

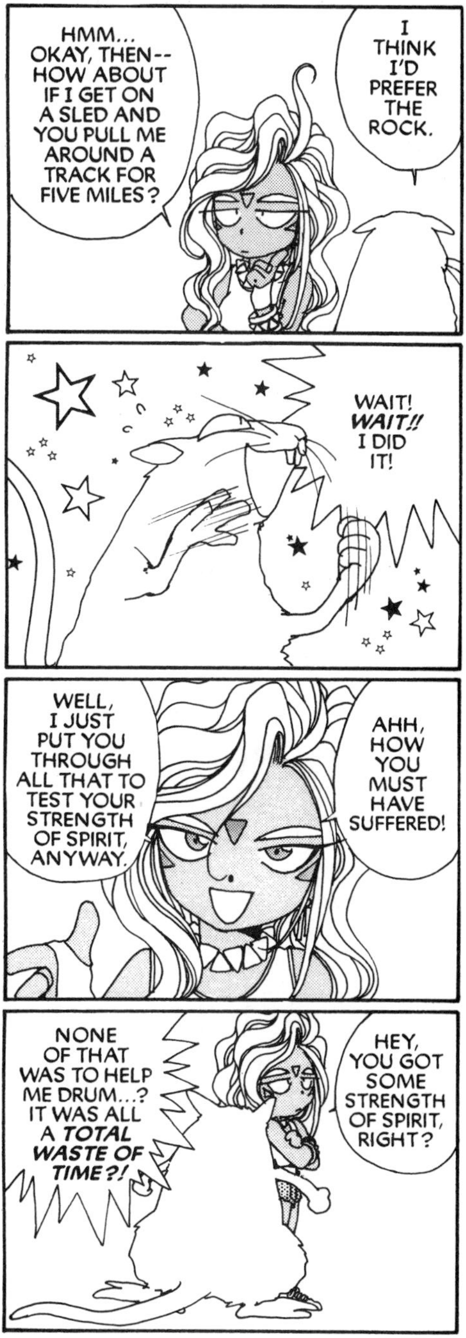
HMM... OKAY, THEN-- HOW ABOUT IF I GET ON A SLED AND YOU PULL ME AROUND A TRACK FOR FIVE MILES?
I THINK I'D PREFER THE ROCK.
WAIT! ***WAIT!!*** I DID IT!
WELL, I JUST PUT YOU THROUGH ALL THAT TO TEST YOUR STRENGTH OF SPIRIT, ANYWAY.
AHH, HOW YOU MUST HAVE SUFFERED!
NONE OF THAT WAS TO HELP ME DRUM...? IT WAS ALL A ***TOTAL WASTE OF TIME?!***
HEY, YOU GOT SOME STRENGTH OF SPIRIT, RIGHT?

SO YOU STARTED A BAND--*NOW* WHAT?

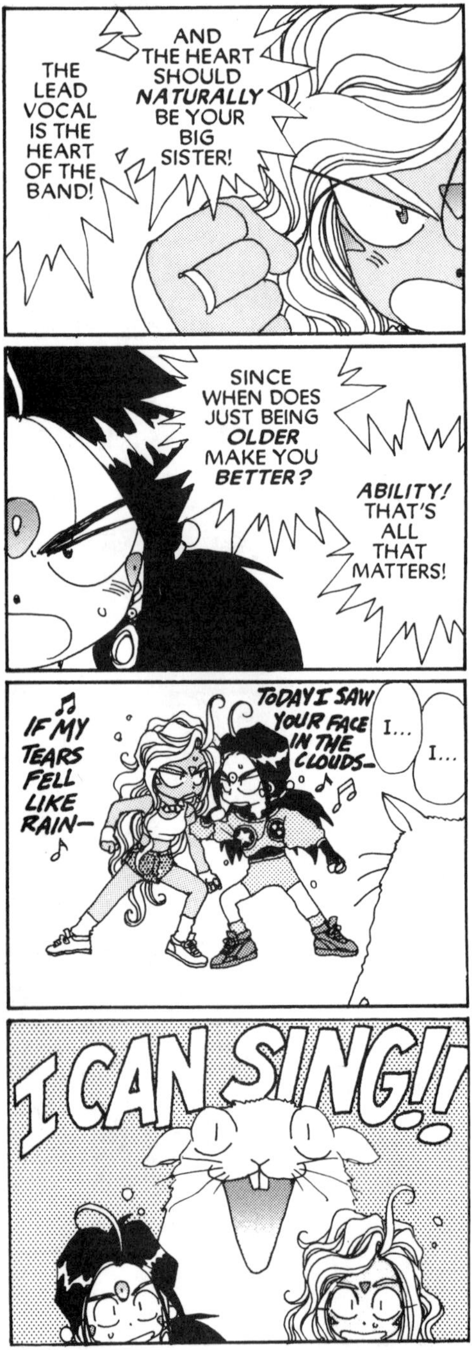

THE LEAD VOCAL IS THE HEART OF THE BAND!
AND THE HEART SHOULD NATURALLY BE YOUR BIG SISTER!
SINCE WHEN DOES JUST BEING OLDER MAKE YOU BETTER?
ABILITY! THAT'S ALL THAT MATTERS!
IF MY TEARS FELL LIKE RAIN-
TODAY I SAW YOUR FACE IN THE CLOUDS-
I...
I...
I CAN SING!!

THE SECRET OF SONG

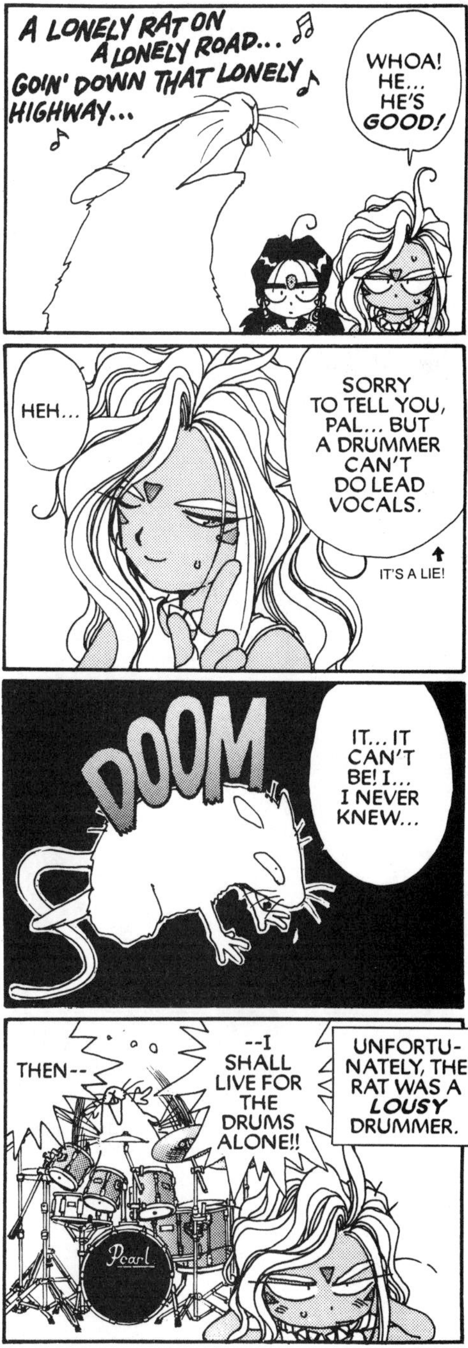
A LONELY RAT ON A LONELY ROAD... GOIN' DOWN THAT LONELY HIGHWAY...
WHOA! HE... HE'S GOOD!
HEH...
SORRY TO TELL YOU, PAL... BUT A DRUMMER CAN'T DO LEAD VOCALS.
IT'S A LIE!
DOOM
IT... IT CAN'T BE! I... I NEVER KNEW...
THEN--
--I SHALL LIVE FOR THE DRUMS ALONE!!
UNFORTUNATELY, THE RAT WAS A LOUSY DRUMMER.
Pearl

REVIVAL! A BAND REBORN!

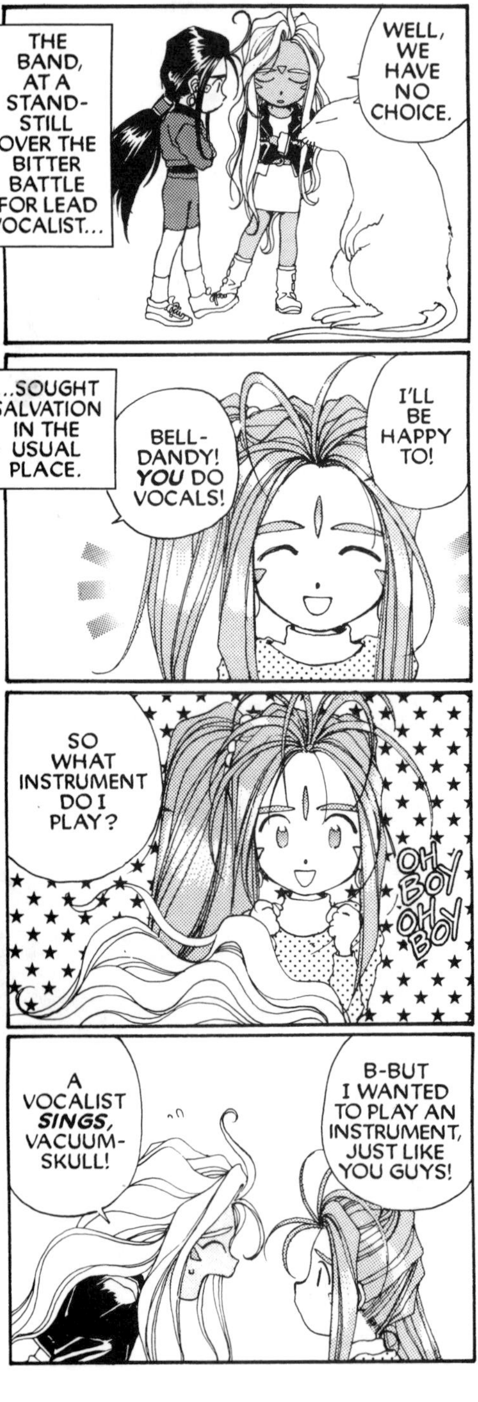
THE BAND, AT A STAND-STILL OVER THE BITTER BATTLE FOR LEAD VOCALIST…
WELL, WE HAVE NO CHOICE.
…SOUGHT SALVATION IN THE USUAL PLACE.
BELL-DANDY! *YOU* DO VOCALS!
I'LL BE HAPPY TO!
SO WHAT INSTRUMENT DO I PLAY?
OH BOY OH BOY
A VOCALIST *SINGS*, VACUUM-SKULL!
B-BUT I WANTED TO PLAY AN INSTRUMENT, JUST LIKE YOU GUYS!

THE INVINCIBLE VOCALIST

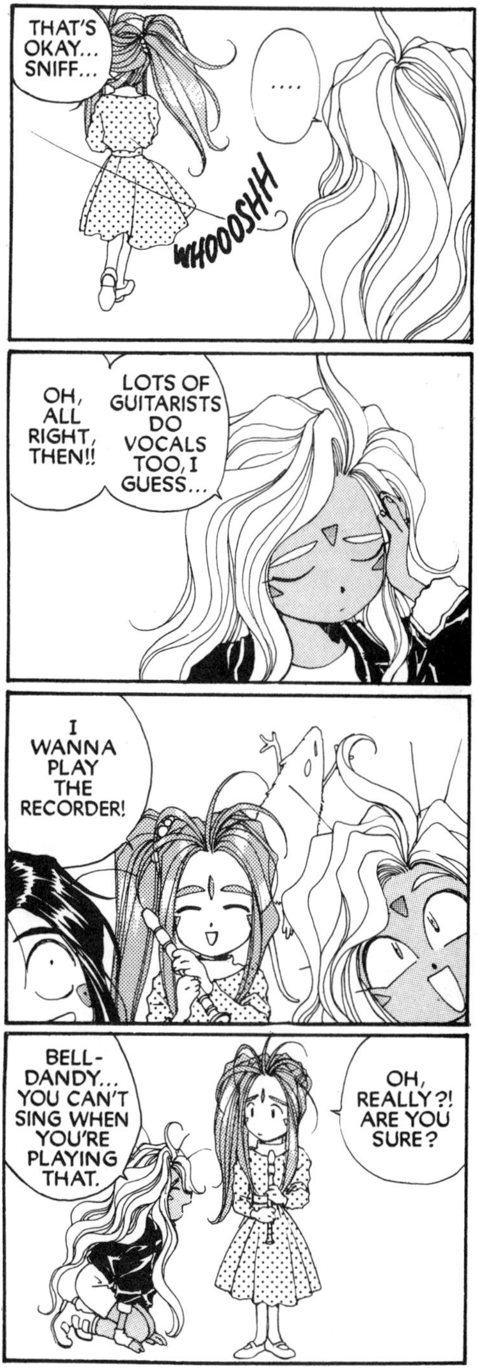
THAT'S OKAY... SNIFF...
....
WHOOOSHH
OH, ALL RIGHT, THEN!!
LOTS OF GUITARISTS DO VOCALS TOO, I GUESS...
I WANNA PLAY THE RECORDER!
BELL-DANDY... YOU CAN'T SING WHEN YOU'RE PLAYING THAT.
OH, REALLY?! ARE YOU SURE?

BACK AGAIN!
THE "OH MY ROCK GODDESS" GRAND PRIX

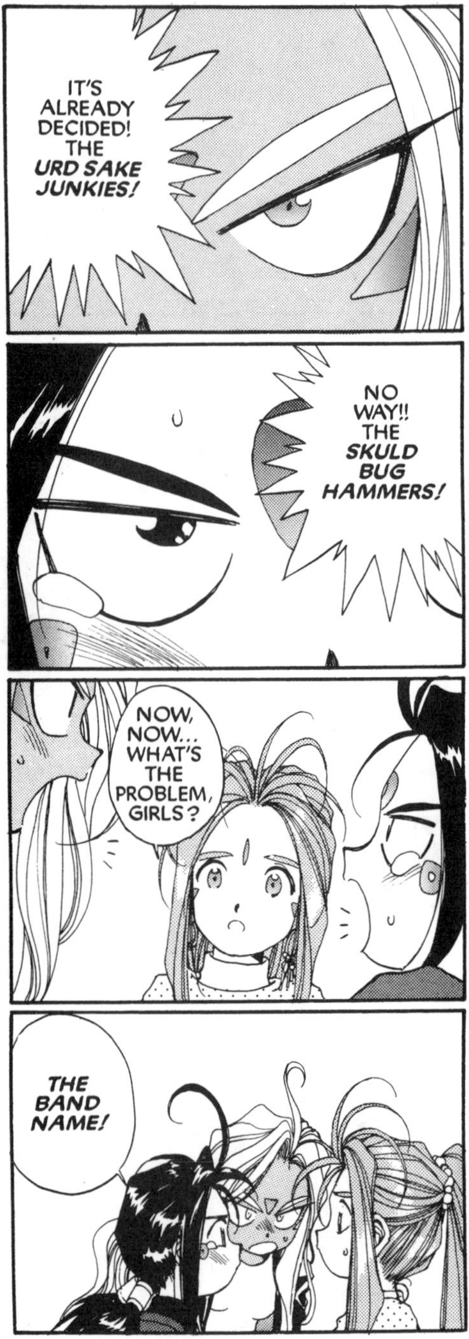
IT'S ALREADY DECIDED! THE URD SAKE JUNKIES!
NO WAY!! THE SKULD BUG HAMMERS!
NOW, NOW... WHAT'S THE PROBLEM, GIRLS?
THE BAND NAME!

BACK AGAIN!
THE "OH MY ROCK GODDESS" GRAND PRIX

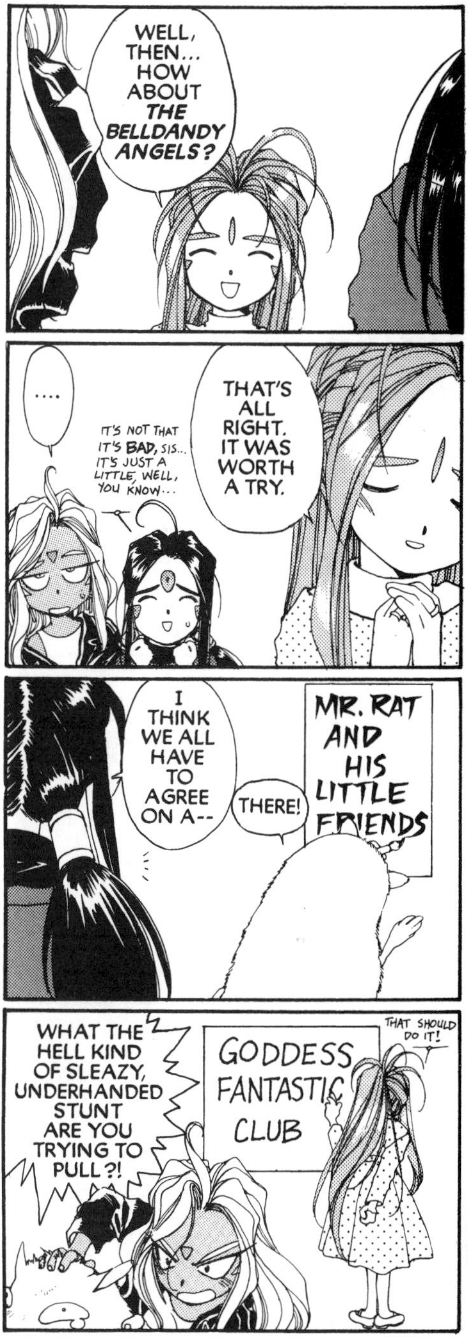
WELL, THEN... HOW ABOUT *THE BELLDANDY ANGELS?*
....
IT'S NOT THAT IT'S BAD, SIS... IT'S JUST A LITTLE, WELL, YOU KNOW...
THAT'S ALL RIGHT. IT WAS WORTH A TRY.
I THINK WE ALL HAVE TO AGREE ON A--
THERE!
MR. RAT AND HIS LITTLE FRIENDS
WHAT THE HELL KIND OF SLEAZY, UNDERHANDED STUNT ARE YOU TRYING TO PULL?!
GODDESS FANTASTIC CLUB
THAT SHOULD DO IT!

▶ PULLING A STUNT OF HER OWN.

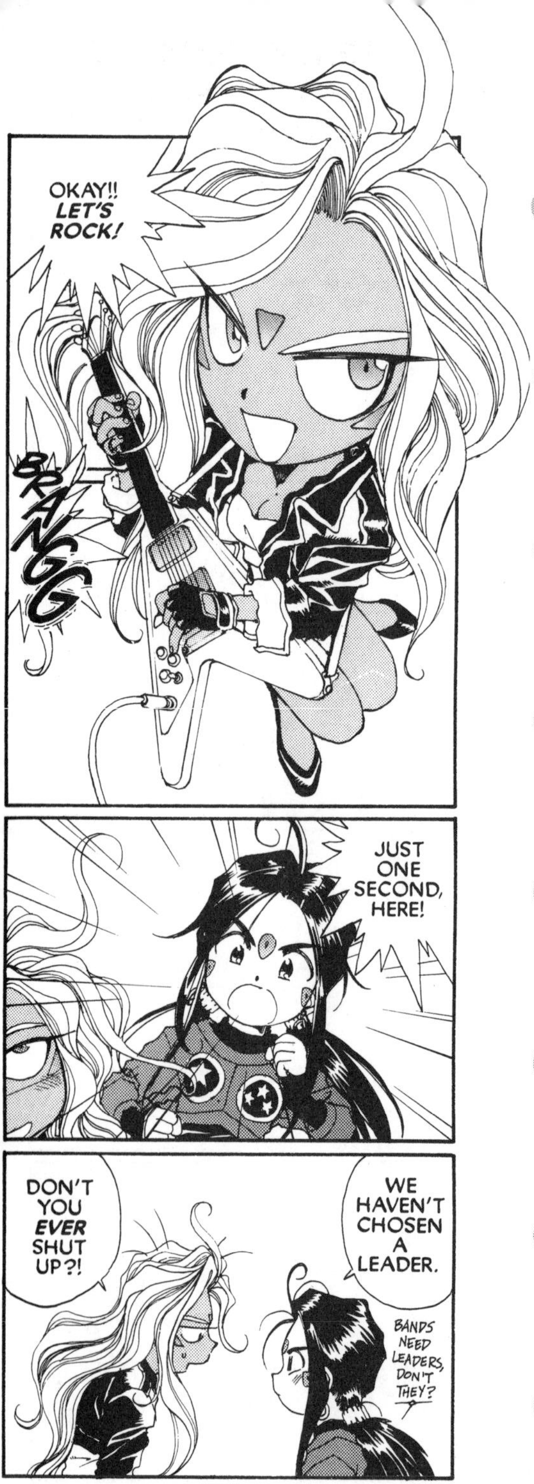
OKAY!! LET'S ROCK!
BRANGG
JUST ONE SECOND, HERE!
DON'T YOU EVER SHUT UP?!
WE HAVEN'T CHOSEN A LEADER.
BANDS NEED LEADERS, DON'T THEY?

THE TRAGIC FLYING "V"! ◆ AND BELLDANDY! ◆ (AND RATTY TOO!)

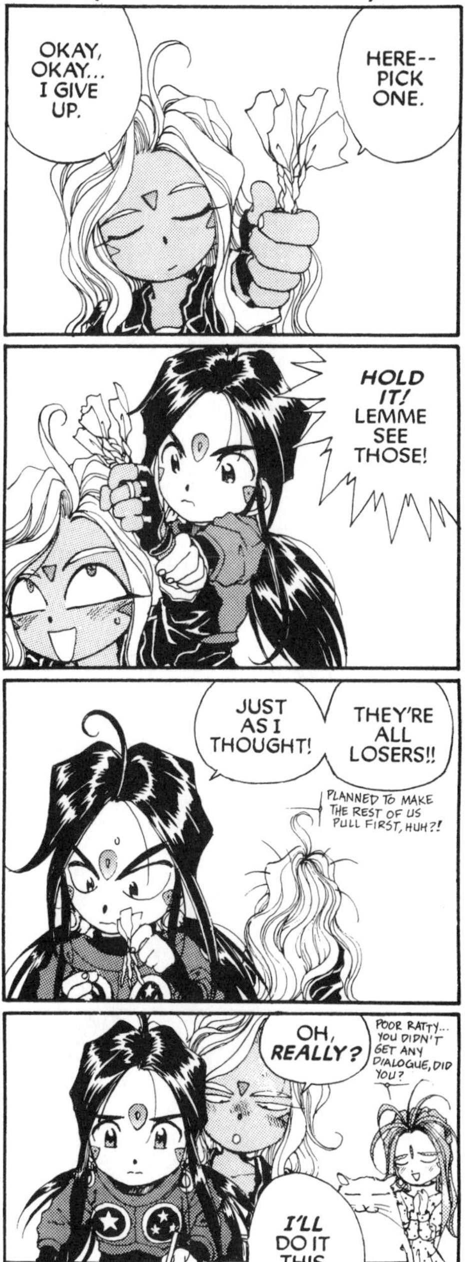
OKAY, OKAY... I GIVE UP.
HERE-- PICK ONE.
HOLD IT! LEMME SEE THOSE!
JUST AS I THOUGHT!
THEY'RE ALL LOSERS!!
PLANNED TO MAKE THE REST OF US PULL FIRST, HUH?!
OH, REALLY?
POOR RATTY... YOU DIDN'T GET ANY DIALOGUE, DID YOU?
I'LL DO IT THIS TIME!

FLY FORTH, ◆ YOUNG SPIRIT! ◆

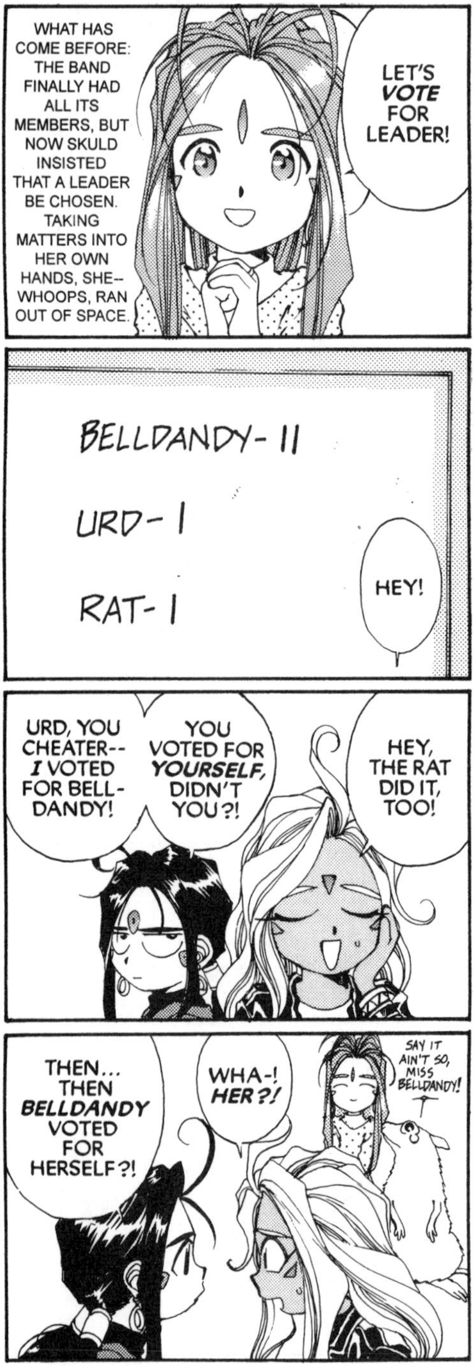

WHAT HAS COME BEFORE: THE BAND FINALLY HAD ALL ITS MEMBERS, BUT NOW SKULD INSISTED THAT A LEADER BE CHOSEN. TAKING MATTERS INTO HER OWN HANDS, SHE-- WHOOPS, RAN OUT OF SPACE.
LET'S *VOTE* FOR LEADER!
BELLDANDY- 11
URD- 1
RAT- 1
HEY!
URD, YOU CHEATER-- *I* VOTED FOR BELL-DANDY!
YOU VOTED FOR *YOURSELF*, DIDN'T YOU?!
HEY, THE RAT DID IT, TOO!
THEN... THEN ***BELLDANDY*** VOTED FOR HERSELF?!
WHA-! *HER?!*
SAY IT AIN'T SO, MISS BELLDANDY!

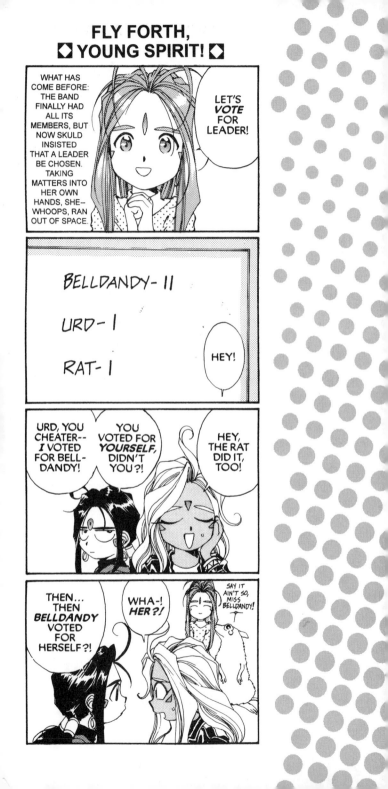

FLY FORTH, YOUNG SPIRIT! (REVISITED)

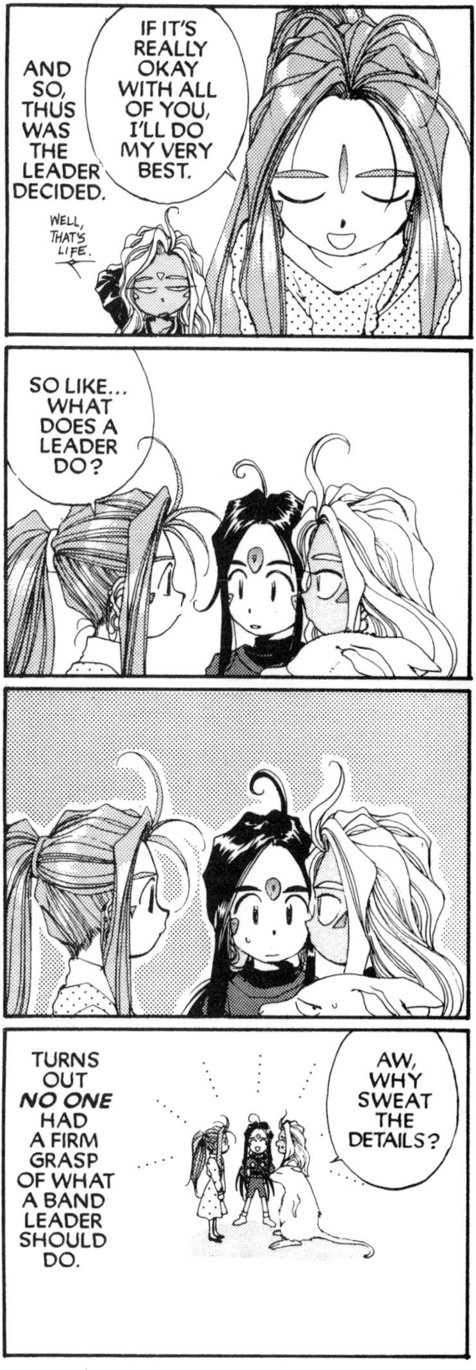
AND SO, THUS WAS THE LEADER DECIDED.
IF IT'S REALLY OKAY WITH ALL OF YOU, I'LL DO MY VERY BEST.
WELL, THAT'S LIFE.
SO LIKE... WHAT DOES A LEADER DO?
TURNS OUT NO ONE HAD A FIRM GRASP OF WHAT A BAND LEADER SHOULD DO.
AW, WHY SWEAT THE DETAILS?

SO YOU WANT TO KNOW MY NAME?!

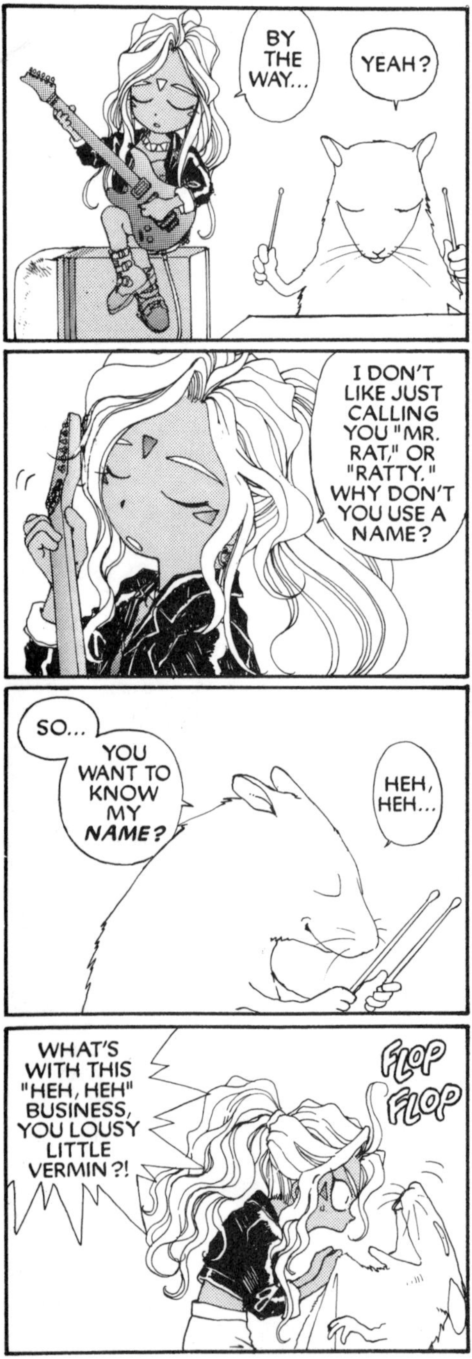
BY THE WAY...
YEAH?
I DON'T LIKE JUST CALLING YOU "MR. RAT," OR "RATTY." WHY DON'T YOU USE A NAME?
SO...
YOU WANT TO KNOW MY *NAME?*
HEH, HEH...
WHAT'S WITH THIS "HEH, HEH" BUSINESS, YOU LOUSY LITTLE VERMIN?!
FLOP
FLOP

THEN I'LL TELL YOU...!

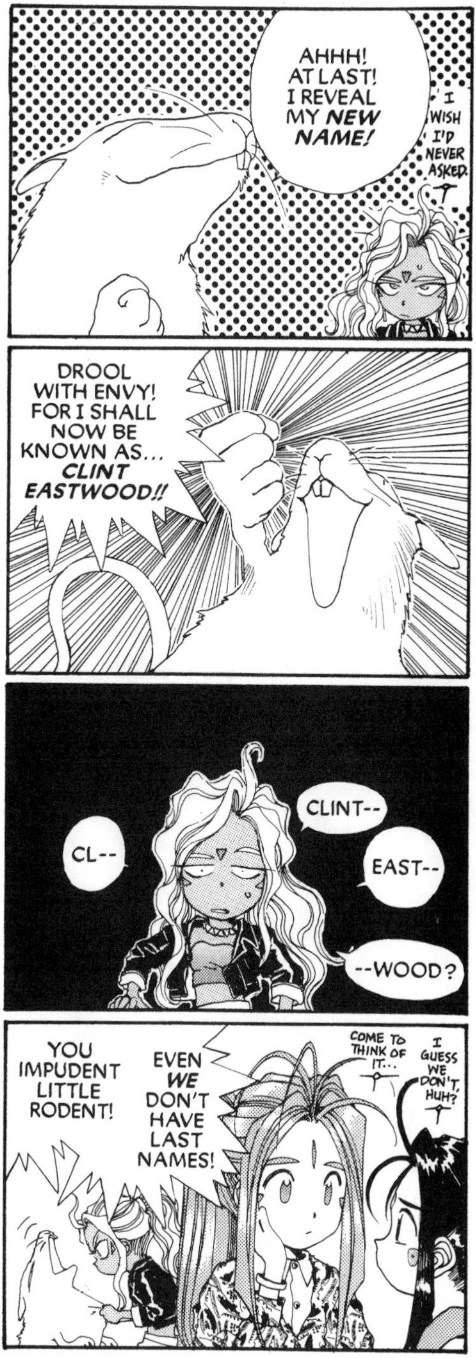
AHHH! AT LAST! I REVEAL MY *NEW NAME!*
I WISH I'D NEVER ASKED.
DROOL WITH ENVY! FOR I SHALL NOW BE KNOWN AS... *CLINT EASTWOOD!!*
CL--
CLINT--
EAST--
--WOOD?
YOU IMPUDENT LITTLE RODENT!
EVEN *WE* DON'T HAVE LAST NAMES!
COME TO THINK OF IT...
I GUESS WE DON'T, HUH?

GAN (AND HIS LITTLE FRIENDS)

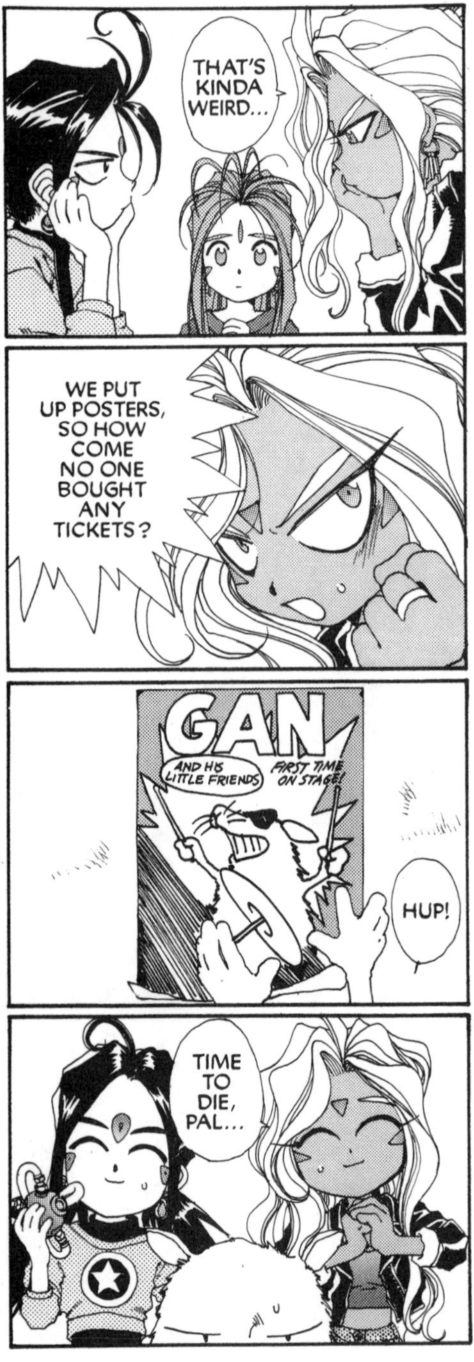
THAT'S KINDA WEIRD...
WE PUT UP POSTERS, SO HOW COME NO ONE BOUGHT ANY TICKETS?
GAN
AND HIS LITTLE FRIENDS
FIRST TIME ON STAGE!
HUP!
TIME TO DIE, PAL...

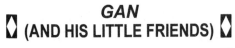

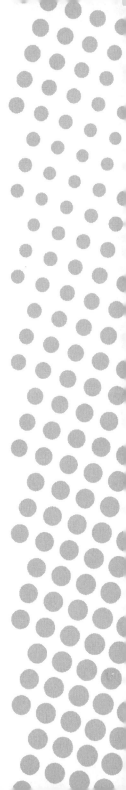

PRIMITIVE ECONOMIC DISTRIBUTION SYSTEMS 101

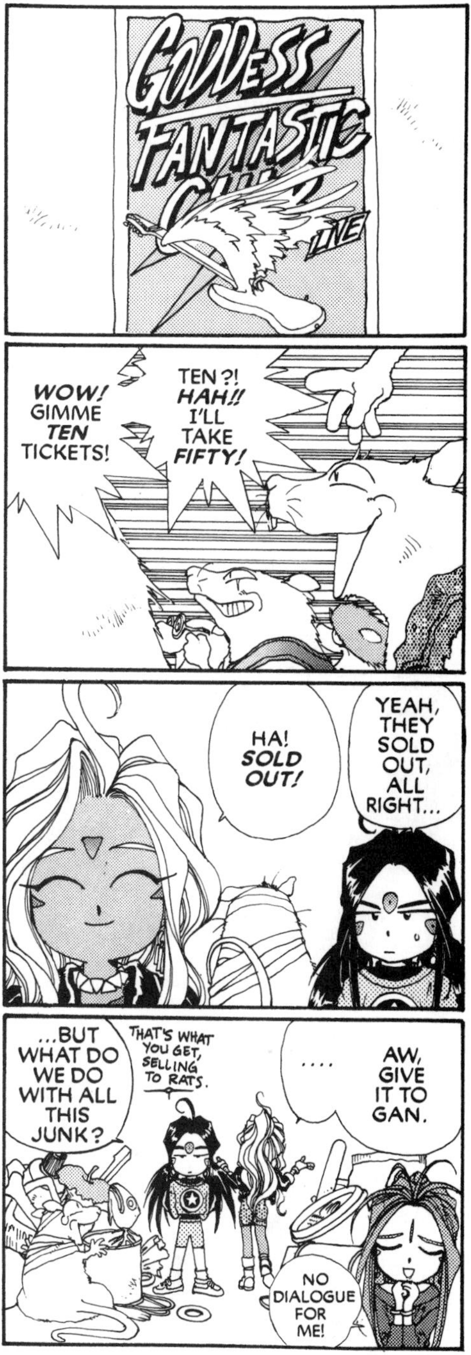
GODDESS
FANTASTIC
LIVE
WOW! GIMME TEN TICKETS!
TEN?! HAH!! I'LL TAKE FIFTY!
HA! SOLD OUT!
YEAH, THEY SOLD OUT, ALL RIGHT...
...BUT WHAT DO WE DO WITH ALL THIS JUNK?
THAT'S WHAT YOU GET, SELLING TO RATS.
....
AW, GIVE IT TO GAN.
NO DIALOGUE FOR ME!

WRITE? WRONG!

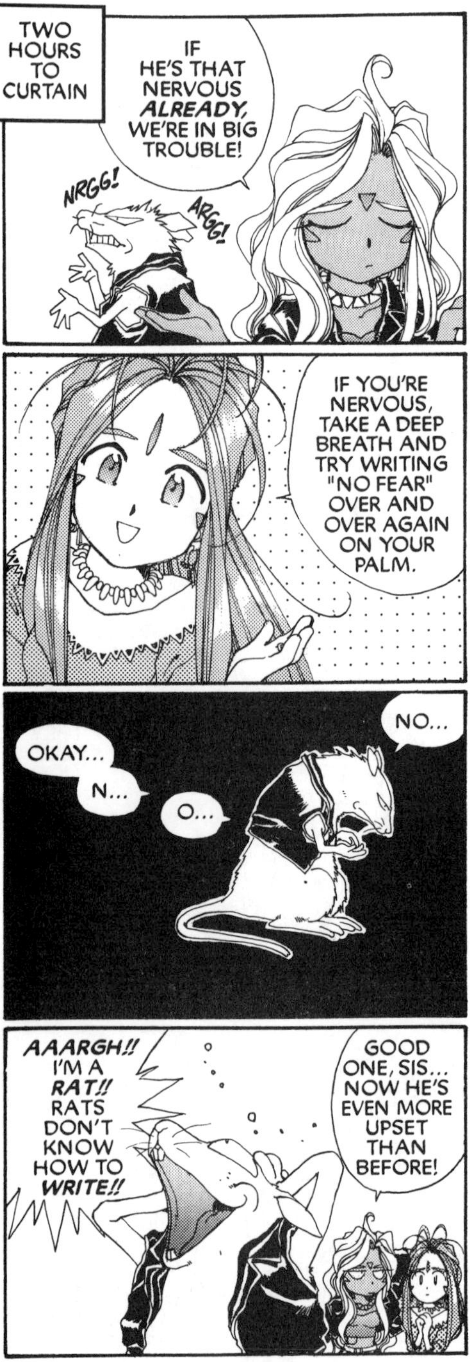

TWO HOURS TO CURTAIN
IF HE'S THAT NERVOUS *ALREADY,* WE'RE IN BIG TROUBLE!
NRGG!
ARGG!
IF YOU'RE NERVOUS, TAKE A DEEP BREATH AND TRY WRITING "NO FEAR" OVER AND OVER AGAIN ON YOUR PALM.
OKAY...
N...
O...
NO...
AAARGH!! I'M A *RAT!!* RATS DON'T KNOW HOW TO *WRITE!!*
GOOD ONE, SIS... NOW HE'S EVEN MORE UPSET THAN BEFORE!

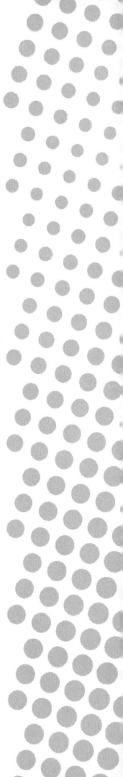

"I'M RUNNING OUT OF PATIENCE..."

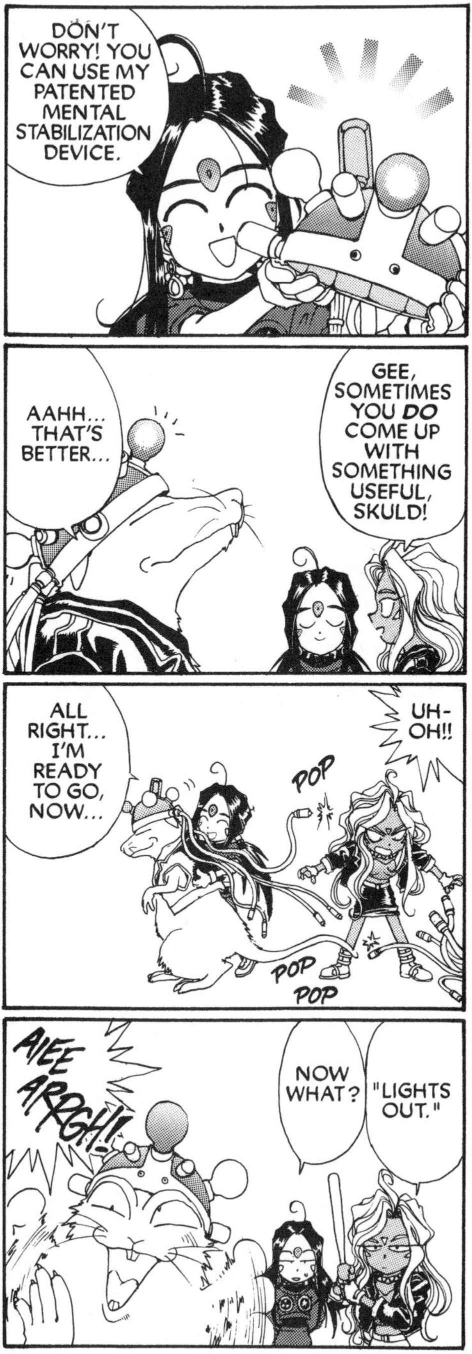
DON'T WORRY! YOU CAN USE MY PATENTED MENTAL STABILIZATION DEVICE.
AAHH... THAT'S BETTER...
GEE, SOMETIMES YOU *DO* COME UP WITH SOMETHING USEFUL, SKULD!
ALL RIGHT... I'M READY TO GO, NOW...
UH-OH!!
POP
POP
POP
AIEE ARRGH!!
NOW WHAT?
"LIGHTS OUT."

SORRY ABOUT THE TINY PRINT IN THE ◇ PLOT SUMMARY... GOOD LUCK! ◇

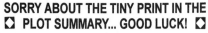

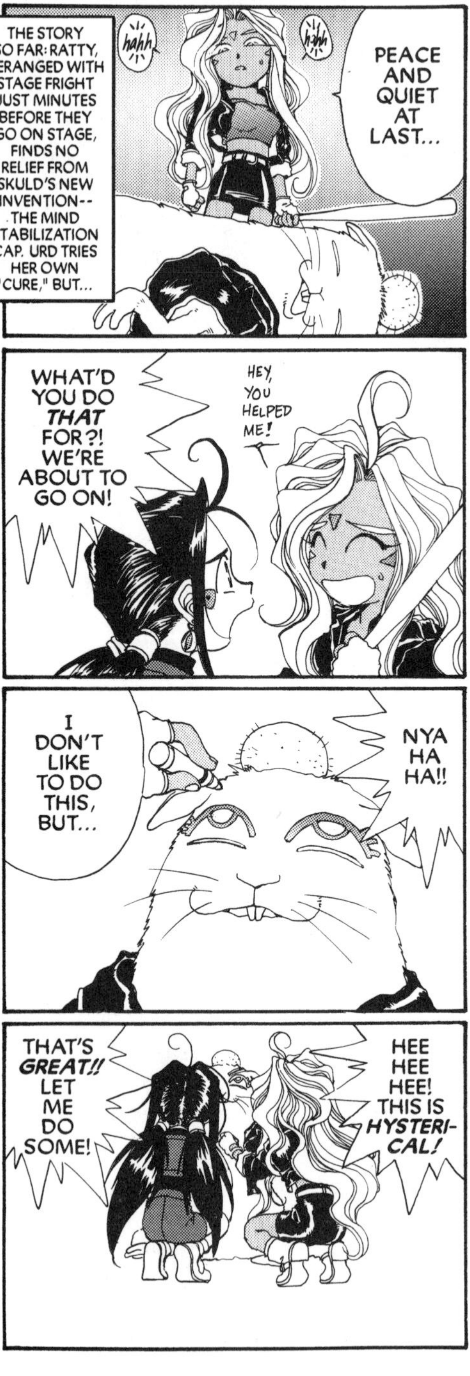
THE STORY SO FAR: RATTY, DERANGED WITH STAGE FRIGHT JUST MINUTES BEFORE THEY GO ON STAGE, FINDS NO RELIEF FROM SKULD'S NEW INVENTION-- THE MIND STABILIZATION CAP. URD TRIES HER OWN "CURE," BUT...
hahh
hahh
PEACE AND QUIET AT LAST...
WHAT'D YOU DO *THAT* FOR?! WE'RE ABOUT TO GO ON!
HEY, YOU HELPED ME!
I DON'T LIKE TO DO THIS, BUT...
NYA HA HA!!
THAT'S *GREAT!!* LET ME DO SOME!
HEE HEE HEE! THIS IS *HYSTERI-CAL!*

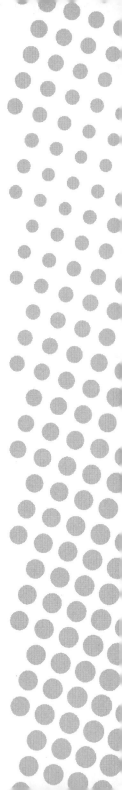

THEIR PURPOSE FORGOTTEN,
THREE GODDESSES AND ONE RAT--
◆ ADRIFT IN THE SEA OF TIME!! ◆

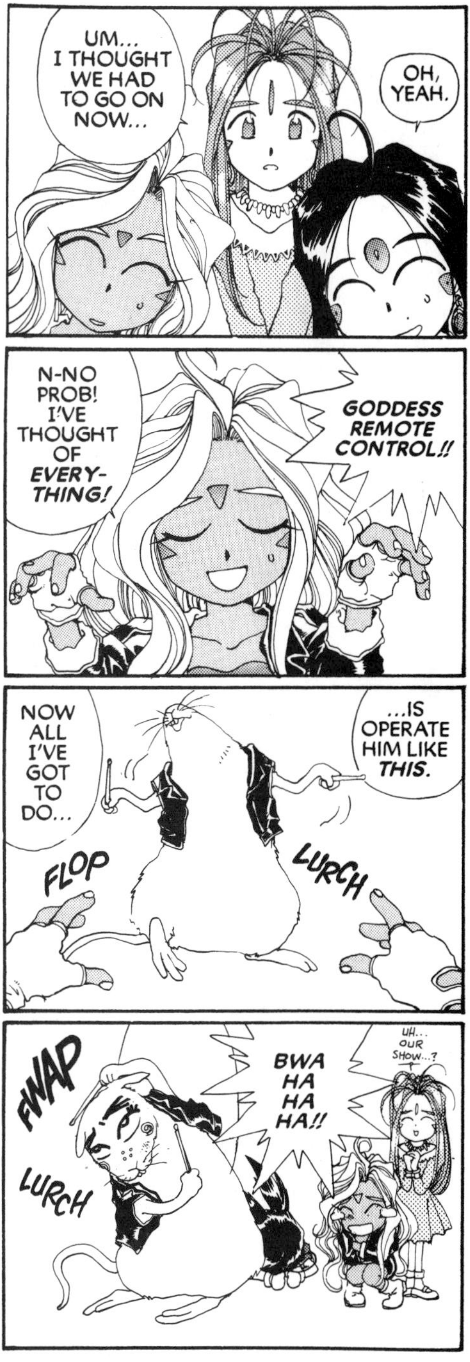

UM... I THOUGHT WE HAD TO GO ON NOW...
OH, YEAH.
N-NO PROB! I'VE THOUGHT OF EVERY-THING!
GODDESS REMOTE CONTROL!!
NOW ALL I'VE GOT TO DO...
...IS OPERATE HIM LIKE THIS.
FLOP
LURCH
FWAP
LURCH
BWA HA HA HA!!
UH... OUR SHOW...?

HEAR THE ROAR OF MY SPIRIT!
SHAKE TO THE BEAT OF MY HEART!
THIS IS ROCK AND ROLL!

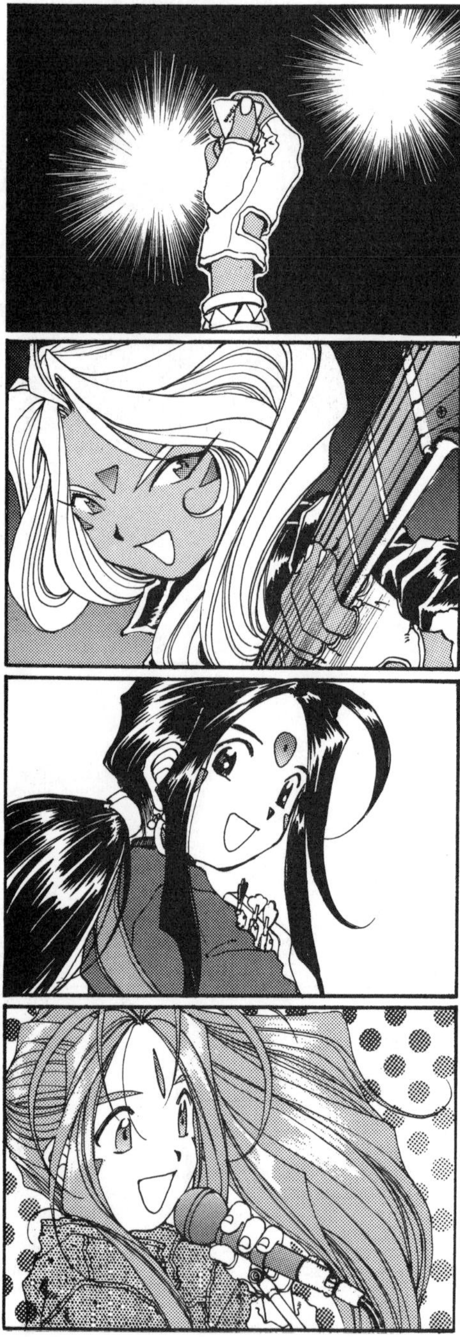

HEAR THE ROAR OF MY SPIRIT!
SHAKE TO THE BEAT OF MY HEART!
THIS IS ROCK AND ROLL!

THE UNCONSCIOUS GAN, STILL BEING REMOTE-CONTROLLED BY URD.
BWA HA HA!
HMM... SO THIS IS ROCK AND ROLL, EH?
NYA HA HA HEE!

MANGA! MANGA! MANGA!
- DARK HORSE HAS THE BEST IN MANGA COLLECTIONS!

AKIRA
Katsuhiro Otomo
BOOK 1
1-56971-498-3 $24.95
BOOK 2
1-56971-499-1 $24.95
BOOK 3
1-56971-525-4 $24.95
BOOK 4
1-56971-526-2 $27.95
BOOK 5
1-56971-527-0 $27.95
BOOK 6
1-56971-528-9 $29.95

APPLESEED
Masamune Shirow
BOOK ONE
1-56971-070-8 $16.95
BOOK TWO
1-56971-071-6 $16.95
BOOK THREE
1-56971-072-4 $17.95
BOOK FOUR
1-56971-074-0 $17.95

BLACK MAGIC
Masamune Shirow
1-56971-360-X $16.95

BLADE OF THE IMMORTAL
Hiroaki Samura
BLOOD OF A THOUSAND
1-56971-239-5 $14.95
CRY OF THE WORM
1-56971-300-6 $14.95
DREAMSONG
1-56971-357-X $14.95
ON SILENT WINGS
1-56971-412-6 $14.95
ON SILENT WINGS II
1-56971-444-4 $14.95
DARK SHADOWS
1-56971-469-X $14.95
HEART OF DARKNESS
1-56971-531-9 $16.95
THE GATHERING
1-56971-546-7 $15.95
THE GATHERING II
1-56971-560-2 $15.95
BEASTS
1-56971-741-9 $14.95

BUBBLEGUM CRISIS
Adam Warren • Toren Smith
GRAND MAL
color paperback
1-56971-120-8 $14.95

CANNON GOD EXAXXION
Kenichi Sonoda
VOLUME 1
1-56971-745-1 $15.95

DOMINION
Masamune Shirow
1-56971-488-6 $16.95

DOMU: A CHILD'S DREAM
Katsuhiro Otomo
1-56971-611-0 $17.95

GHOST IN THE SHELL
Masamune Shirow
color/B&W paperback
1-56971-081-3 $24.95

GUNSMITH CATS
Kenichi Sonoda
BONNIE AND CLYDE
1-56971-215-8 $13.95
MISFIRE
1-56971-253-0 $14.95
THE RETURN OF GRAY
1-56971-299-9 $17.95
GOLDIE VS. MISTY
1-56971-371-5 $15.95
BAD TRIP
1-56971-442-8 $13.95
BEAN BANDIT
1-56971-453-3 $16.95
KIDNAPPED
1-56971-529-7 $16.95
MISTER V
1-56971-550-5 $18.95
MISTY'S RUN
1-56971-684-6 $14.95

INTRON DEPOT
Masamune Shirow
INTRON DEPOT 1
1-56971-085-6 $39.95
INTRON DEPOT 2: BLADES
1-56971-382-0 $39.95

LONE WOLF & CUB
Kazuo Koike and Goseki Kojima
VOLUME 1:
THE ASSASSIN'S ROAD
1-56971-502-5 $9.95
VOLUME 2:
THE GATELESS BARRIER
1-56971-503-3 $9.95
VOLUME 3: THE FLUTE
OF THE FALLEN TIGER
1-56971-504-1 $9.95
VOLUME 4:
THE BELL WARDEN
1-56971-505-X $9.95
VOLUME 5:
BLACK WIND
1-56971-506-8 $9.95
VOLUME 6:
LANTERNS FOR THE DEAD
1-56971-507-6 $9.95
VOLUME 7:
CLOUD DRAGON, WIND TIGER
1-56971-508-4 $9.95
VOLUME 8:
CHAINS OF DEATH
1-56971-509-2 $9.95
VOLUME 9:
ECHO OF THE ASSASSIN
1-56971-510-6 $9.95
VOLUME 10:
HOSTAGE CHILD
1-56971-511-4 $9.95
VOLUME 11:
TALISMAN OF HADES
1-56971-512-2 $9.95
VOLUME 12:
SHATTERED STONES
1-56971-513-0 $9.95
VOLUME 13:
THE MOON IN THE EAST,
THE SUN IN THE WEST
1-56971-585-8 $9.95
VOLUME 14:
DAY OF THE DEMONS
1-56971-586-6 $9.95
VOLUME 15:
BROTHERS OF THE GRASS
1-56971-587-4 $9.95
VOLUME 16:
GATEWAY INTO WINTER
1-56971-588-2 $9.95
VOLUME 17:
THE WILL OF THE FANG
1-56971-589-0 $9.95
VOLUME 18:
TWILIGHT OF
THE KUROKUWA
1-56971-590-4 $9.95
VOLUME 19:
THE MOON IN OUR HEARTS
1-56971-591-2 $9.95
VOLUME 20:
A TASTE OF POISON
1-56971-592-0 $9.95
VOLUME 21:
FRAGRANCE OF DEATH
1-56971-593-9 $9.95
VOLUME 22:
HEAVEN AND EARTH
1-56971-594-7 $9.95
VOLUME 23:
TEARS OF ICE
1-56971-595-5 $9.95
VOLUME 24:
IN THESE SMALL HANDS
1-56971-596-3 $9.95
VOLUME 25:
PERHAPS IN DEATH
1-56971-597-1 $9.95
VOLUME 26:
STRUGGLE IN THE DARK
1-56971-598-X $9.95
VOLUME 27:
BATTLE'S EVE
1-56971-599-8 $9.95
VOLUME 28:
THE LOTUS THRONE
1-56971-600-5 $9.95

OH MY GODDESS!
Kosuke Fujishima
WRONG NUMBER
1-56971-669-2 $13.95
LOVE POTION NO. 9
1-56971-252-2 $14.95
SYMPATHY FOR THE DEVIL
1-56971-329-4 $13.95
TERRIBLE MASTER URD
1-56971-369-3 $14.95
ADVENTURES OF
THE MINI-GODDESSES
1-56971-421-5 $9.95
THE QUEEN OF VENGEANCE
1-56971-431-2 $13.95
MARA STRIKES BACK!
1-56971-449-5 $14.95
NINJA MASTER
1-56971-474-6 $13.95
MISS KEIICHI
1-56971-522-X $16.95
THE DEVIL IN MISS URD
1-56971-540-8 $14.95
THE FOURTH GODDESS
1-56971-551-3 $18.95
CHILDHOOD'S END
1-56971-685-4 $15.95
QUEEN SAYOKO
1-56971-766-4 $16.95
HAND IN HAND TP
1-56971-921-7 $17.95
MYSTERY CHILD
1-56971-950-0 $17.95

SERAPHIC FEATHER
Hiroyuki Utatane • Yo Morimoto
VOLUME 1:
CRIMSON ANGEL
1-56971-555-6 $17.95
VOLUME 2:
SEEDS OF CHAOS
1-56971-739-7 $17.95

SHADOW STAR
Mohiro Kitoh
VOLUME 1:
STARFLIGHT
1-56971-548-3 $15.95
VOLUME 2:
DARKNESS VISIBLE
1-56971-740-0 $14.95
VOLUME 3:
SHADOWS OF THE PAST
1-56971-743-5 $13.95

3X3 EYES
Yuzo Takada
HOUSE OF DEMONS
1-56971-930-6 $12.95
CURSE OF THE GESU
1-56971-931-4 $12.95
FLIGHT OF THE DEMON
1-56971-553-X $15.95
BLOOD OF
THE SACRED DEMON
1-56971-735-4 $13.95
SUMMONING OF THE BEAST
1-56971-747-8 $14.95

WHAT'S MICHAEL?
Makoto Kobayashi
BOOK 5:
WHAT'S MICHAEL'S
FAVORITE SPOT?
1-56971-557-2 $8.95
BOOK 6:
HARD DAY'S LIFE
1-56971-744-3 $8.95

Available from your local comics shop or bookstore!

To find a comics shop in your area, call 1-888-266-4226

For more information or to order direct: •On the web: www.darkhorse.com •E-mail: mailorder@darkhorse.com •Phone: 1-800-862-0052 or (503) 652-9701 Mon.-Sat. 9 A.M. to 5 P.M. Pacific Time